"Many would have us believe that life is hopelessly fragmented and truth an elusive dream. The authors of this book beg to differ and enthusiastically point us to the cohesive centrality and absolute supremacy of Jesus Christ. Having heard these messages live at the 2006 Desiring God National Conference, I'm thrilled to see them now in print. Highly recommended!"

—SAM STORMS, founder, Enjoying God Ministries

"Over the past decade evangelicals have been divided over how to respond to the challenges of postmodernism. The options—which have ranged from naïve denial to unquestioned embrace—tend to suffer from the same fatal flaw: putting the emphasis on culture rather than on Christ. This collection corrects that error by providing a fresh perspective that is pastorally sensitive and biblically sound. A timely, well-reasoned book that should be enthusiastically welcomed by the evangelical community."

—JOE CARTER, blogger(www.evangelicaloutpost.com); director of communications, Family Research Council

# The Supremacy of Christ in a Postmodern World

Crossway books co-edited by
**JOHN PIPER and JUSTIN TAYLOR:**

*Suffering and the Sovereignty of God* (2006)

*Sex and the Supremacy of Christ* (2005)

*A God-Entranced Vision of All Things:*
*The Legacy of Jonathan Edwards* (2004)

*Beyond the Bounds:*
*Open Theism and the Undermining of Biblical Christianity* (2003)

# The Supremacy of Christ
## in a Postmodern World

# John Piper | Justin Taylor

### GENERAL EDITORS

## CROSSWAY BOOKS
### WHEATON, ILLINOIS

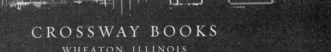

*The Supremacy of Christ in a Postmodern World*

Copyright © 2007 by Desiring God Ministries

Published by Crossway Books
      a publishing ministry of Good News Publishers
      1300 Crescent Street
      Wheaton, Illinois 60187

Cover photo: iStock

First printing 2007

Printed in the United States of America

Unless otherwise indicated, Scripture quotations are from *The Holy Bible, English Standard Version,*® copyright © 2001 by Crossway Bibles, a publishing ministry of Good News Publishers. Used by permission. All rights reserved.

Scripture quotations marked NASB are from *The New American Standard Bible.*® Copyright © The Lockman Foundation 1960, 1962, 1963, 1968, 1971, 1972, 1973, 1975, 1977, 1995. Used by permission.

Scripture references marked NIV are from *The Holy Bible: New International Version.*® Copyright © 1973, 1978, 1984 by International Bible Society. Used by permission of Zondervan Publishing House. All rights reserved.

The "NIV" and "New International Version" trademarks are registered in the United States Patent and Trademark Office by International Bible Society. Use of either trademark requires the permission of International Bible Society.

Scripture quotations marked KJV are from the King James Version of the Bible.

All emphases in Scripture quotations have been added by the author.

**Library of Congress Cataloging-in-Publication Data**
The Supremacy of Christ in a postmodern world / John Piper and
Justin Taylor, editors.
    p. cm.
    Includes index.
    ISBN 978-1-58134-922-1 (tpb)
    1. Apologetics. 2. Jesus Christ—Person and offices. 3. Postmodernism—
Religious aspects—Christianity. I. Piper, John, 1946–    . II. Taylor, Justin,
1976–   . III. Title.
BT1103.S87     2007
230—dc22                       2007024825

BP       17  16  15  14  13  12  11  10  09  08  07
15  14  13  12  11  10  9  8  7  6  5  4  3  2  1

To
JOHN STOTT

*for faithfully cherishing and proclaiming
the supremacy of Christ
in all things*

# Contents

# Contributors

**Voddie Baucham Jr.,** pastor of preaching at Grace Family Baptist Church, Spring, Texas.

**D. A. Carson,** research professor of New Testament, Trinity Evangelical Divinity School, Deerfield, Illinois.

**Mark Driscoll,** preaching pastor, Mars Hill Church, Seattle, Washington.

**Tim Keller,** senior pastor, Redeemer Presbyterian Church, New York, New York.

**John Piper,** pastor for preaching and vision, Bethlehem Baptist Church, Minneapolis, Minnesota.

**Justin Taylor,** associate publisher and Study Bible project director, Crossway Bibles, Wheaton, Illinois.

**David Wells,** Andrew Mutch distinguished professor of historical and systematic theology, Gordon-Conwell Theological Seminary, South Hamilton, Massachusetts.

# Introduction

JUSTIN TAYLOR

The chapters in this volume grow out of a conference convened in Minneapolis in the fall of 2006 to explore the supremacy of Christ in a postmodern world. The speakers at that conference—and now the contributors to this volume—were David Wells, Voddie Baucham Jr., John Piper, D. A. Carson, Tim Keller, and Mark Driscoll. Whether addressing culture, truth, joy, love, the gospel, or the church, each seeks to sharpen our thinking and motivate our ministry by considering how each of these intersects with the truth of Christ in our contemporary world.

What follows is a brief overview of each chapter.

## Culture and Truth

David Wells observes that two realities are currently transforming culture: the emergence of the postmodern ethos and the tidal wave of ethnic and religious diversity in the West. These two motifs are changing the cultural context within which the church is to live, move, and have its being. Theology, if true to its nature, must be missional, and, therefore, we must seek to understand both Christ and culture, both the Word and the world. Wells goes on to explore two ways in which postmodern belief is expressing itself in this cultural context: through a form of spirituality that distinguishes itself from being religious and through the language of meaninglessness, whereby reality is collapsed into the self. Wells then addresses how the supremacy of Christ and biblical reality speak into both situations.

Voddie Baucham Jr. addresses life's ultimate questions from the perspective of two broad worldviews: Christian theism and a postmodern version of secular humanism. He first gives a cursory overview of these systems by means of five major categories: (1) God; (2) man; (3) truth; (4) knowledge; and (5) ethics. He then explores how these competing perspectives work in terms of life's ultimate questions: (1) Who am I? (2) Why am I here? (3) What is wrong with the world? and (4) How can what is wrong be made right? Using Colossians 1:12–21 as a framework, he shows the supremacy of Christ in truth over against a dying, decaying, and hurting postmodern world.

## Joy and Love

John Piper's chapter is built on John 17:13—"But now I am coming to you, and these things I speak in the world, that they may have my joy fulfilled in themselves." Piper suggests that the deepest source of this joy is Jesus' seeing and sharing the Father's glory, and that this joy is conveyed to us through propositions. Piper's arguments proceed logically through ten steps: (1) God is the only eternal being; therefore everything and everyone else is dependent on, and less valuable than, him. (2) God has been eternally and supremely joyful in the fellowship of the Trinity, so he has no deficiency that would prompt him to create the world. (3) God created human beings in his own image so that his glory might be displayed by being known and enjoyed by them. (4) Christ came into the world and accomplished his work so that all who receive Jesus as their Savior, Lord, and Treasure would be justified and fitted to know and enjoy God forever. (5) The enjoyment of God above all else is the deepest way that God's glory is reflected to, and terminates on, God. (6) Nevertheless, God has constituted us so that our enjoyment of him overflows in visible acts of love to others. (7) The only God-glorifying love and joy is rooted in the true knowledge of God. (8) Therefore, the right knowledge of God and his ways is the servant of God-glorifying joy in him and love for people. (9) Therefore healthy biblical doctrine should not be marginalized or minimized, but rather embraced and cherished as the basis for building friendships and churches. (10) And, thus, the church should become that for which it was created, namely, the pillar and buttress of truth, joy, and love in order to display the glory of God and the supremacy of Christ in all things.

Whereas Piper's chapter focuses on one of the petitions from John 17, D. A. Carson's chapter examines all five of the petitions Jesus offers for his followers, namely, that God the Father will (1) keep them safe; (2) make them one; (3) and sanctify them; and that his followers will

(4) experience the full measure of Jesus' own joy; and (5) be with him forever. Carson also identifies each petition's ground or reason, purpose, and connection to the theme of love. He then connects all of this with the supremacy of Christ and how it relates to Christ's love for the Father and for us. He closes by briefly considering how other voices—those of critical scholarship, ecumenism, and postmodernism—respond to these truths. Fittingly, the chapter closes in the language of biblical worship.

## Gospel Theologizing and Contextualizing

Tim Keller suggests that our current cultural situation poses a crisis for the way evangelicals have been doing evangelism for the past 150 years, causing us to raise crucial questions like: How do we do evangelism today? How do we get the gospel across in a postmodern world? Keller believes that we need to rethink our ordinary way of doing ministry due to the cultural changes (especially in secularized Europe and places in the United States that are similar) and the fact that the church is now on a mission field. He proposes six ways that the church has to change, finding parallels in Jonah and his mission to the great pagan metropolis of Nineveh. Keller calls these six factors (1) gospel theologizing (*all* of theology must be an exposition of the gospel); (2) gospel realizing (we can "know" the gospel and yet not truly *know* the gospel); (3) gospel urbanizing (many Christians must move to the city, urbanize the gospel, and create strong versions of gospel communities); (4) gospel communication (through evangelism that is intelligible, credible, plausible, thorough, progressive, and process-oriented); (5) gospel humiliation (Christ's power is evident through your weakness); and (6) gospel incarnation (within a pagan city God's people are to be neither withdrawn nor assimilated but, rather, distinct and engaged). In conclusion, Keller asks if we might be insulting God with our small ambitions and low expectations for evangelism today.

Mark Driscoll begins his chapter by noting the ways in which Jesus continues to be used in pop culture. With regard to the historical Christ, he suggests that liberals and Emergents have overemphasized the incarnation/humanity of Jesus at the expense of the exaltation/divinity of Jesus. Conversely, Jesus' exaltation/divinity is overemphasized by conservatives and fundamentalists at the expense of his incarnation/humanity. Driscoll argues that both truths must be equally emphasized. Driscoll goes on to argue for a "two-handed approach to Christian ministry" whereby the timeless truths of Christianity are held in a firmly closed hand, and timely ministry methods and styles are held loosely in a gracious open hand. Among the truths for which we must *contend* are (1) Scripture as inerrant, timeless truth; (2) the sovereignty and foreknowledge of God; (3) the virgin birth of Jesus; (4) our sin nature and total depravity; (5) Jesus' death as our penal substitution; (6) Jesus' exclusivity as the only possible means of salvation; (7) God-designed complementary male and female gender distinctions; (8) the conscious eternal torments of hell; (9) the preeminence of God's kingdom over human culture; and (10) the recognition that Satan and demons are real and at work in the world. Once we have rightly understood these truths, we are then ready to *contextualize* Christian belief and practice to varying cultures and subcultures. Driscoll closes by showing that this was the very strategy of Calvin's church-planting philosophy and program.

### Conversations with the Contributors

The final section of the book contains interviews conducted with the contributors, allowing them to flesh out some of their points and to address issues not covered in their chapters.

### Our Prayer

In submitting this work for publication and entrusting it now to you, the reader, our hope is that you will find in these pages material that both edifies and instructs. Not every chapter has to be read—certainly not in order. But our prayer is that God would use these essays—for his glory and for your good—to meet your needs and to edify the church of Jesus Christ as we seek to "contend for the faith that was once for all delivered to the saints" (Jude 3) and simultaneously "become all things to all people, that by all means [we] might save some . . . for the sake of the gospel" (1 Cor. 9:22–23).

### Acknowledgements

We wish to thank several people who have helped us with this project. Without Jon Bloom (the executive director at Desiring God) and Scott Anderson (the conference director), there would have been no conference and, therefore, no book. We are thankful to Crossway Books—especially Lane Dennis and Allan Fisher—not only for publishing this book but for believing in and promoting the vision of God and ministry that it embodies. David Mathis and Sherah Baumgarten have helped time and again with excellent administrative and editorial assistance. Lydia Brownback skillfully edited the book under a tight timeline, and Carol Steinbach once again lent her expertise in creating the indexes that serve readers so well. Our wives, Noël Piper and Lea Taylor, have made our homes a pleasant place to be and have served us through their servant-heart patience and encouragement.

We have dedicated this book to John Stott, who retired from public ministry at the age of 86 in July of 2007. John is a faithful student of both Christ and culture, and we honor the legacy of his Christ-exalting ministry, in both word and deed.

Part 1

# Culture and Truth

# CHAPTER 1

## The Supremacy of Christ in a Postmodern World

DAVID WELLS

Tuesday, September 11, 2001.[1] The weather in Boston was clear, the sky cloudless, the air crisp, the trees showing just the first hint of fall color. That was the day that two jets left Logan International Airport for California but were hijacked and, a short time later, flown into the towers of the World Trade Center in New York. Thousands of people who thought they were beginning another ordinary day were killed in an extraordinary way. Two other jets were also hijacked that day, one ending up in the side of the Pentagon and the other in a field in Pennsylvania, the latter thanks to brave, bare-handed, anti-terrorist action on board. On that day the United States suffered its worst act of terrorism, a ghastly moment of cold, callous, calculated mass murder. It left a gaping hole in the nation's heart and images of chaos and wreckage etched forever in its memory.

In the days that followed, as dazed Americans watched the pictures from the crash scenes, the distractions that make up the noisy surface where we live were stripped away. It is, of course, the rather mundane routines and events of life that give it a sense of daily normalcy. But these were not normal days, and much of the surface clutter simply stopped. It suddenly seemed indecent, inappropriate, in light of this stark, unrelieved tragedy.

Television cleansed itself of its incessant barrage of commercials

---

[1] This chapter is adapted from David F. Wells, *Above All Earthly Pow'rs: Christ in a Postmodern World* (Grand Rapids, MI: Eerdmans, 2005). Used with permission.

and, for a few days, offered uninterrupted coverage of the unfolding events. And how could we ponder this appalling loss and, at the same time, sit back to watch the Miss America beauty pageant or the Emmy Awards? They were canceled. The late-night comedians fled the air. Hollywood studios were quick to finger this pulse and revisited their decisions regarding what movies would be released in the fall. Even the usual bickering and destructiveness of the political process, driven by the competition for power and ever feasting on the nation's social divisions, stopped overnight. National purpose now loomed over these squabbles. It suddenly—and unusually—seemed to be a bigger thing than narrow, partisan interest. Indeed, the politicians seemed almost to have been shamed into attending to matters of national concern.

At all the crash scenes, but especially in New York, onlookers gazed in sad awe at the smoking wreckage, buildings and planes twisted into grotesque shapes and hiding within them the crushed bodies of those taken down. The nation's attention was simultaneously riveted on the heroic actions of those who worked with such determination, and amidst such tiredness, to find any who might still be alive. Here, too, was another telling juxtaposition: the terrorists' dark hatred and the remarkable bravery and fortitude of those who continued to dig for the lost.

This event, which was so unexpected, so terrible, and so psychologically intrusive, brought into clearer focus a number of other issues. Three of them are particularly germane to this present discussion. First of all, there is the fact that for all of the talk about how America changed after this event, there remains an uneasy sense that American culture is actually little different from what it was before—that it still is morally and spiritually adrift, and in this it is no different from the other Western countries. Second, the global ambitions of radical Islam called attention to the many Muslims in the West and this, in turn, was a reminder of the West's growing ethnic and religious complexity. To this America is no exception for, in a short period of time, it has become the world's most religiously diverse nation. Third, this moment of tragedy and evil shone its own light on the church, and what we came to see was not a happy sight. For what has become conspicuous by its scarcity, and not least in the evangelical corner of it, is a spiritual *gravitas*, one that could match the depth of horrendous evil and address issues of such seriousness. Evangelicalism, now much absorbed by the arts and tricks of marketing, is simply not very serious anymore.

**The Front Lines**

These three issues do, of course, have their connections. The first two, I believe, are the major defining cultural realities with which the church must now intentionally engage: first, the disintegration of the Enlightenment world and its replacement by the postmodern ethos and, second, the fact that through the changed immigration law of 1965, America has become a truly multiethnic society and perhaps the most religiously diverse one in the world. The exotic religions from faraway places that once only filled the pages of *National Geographic* may now be next door. Mosques, landmarks that once seemed confined to the Middle East, can now be seen side-by-side with churches in America, though much of the practice of Islam is invisible to most people. America is now home to more Hispanics than African Americans; Arabs are coming close to drawing even with Jews in number; and there are more Muslims than Episcopalians, or Congregationalists, or Eastern Orthodox, or Mormons. The arrival of old, non-Christian religions in America and the emergence of more recent spiritualities that are not religious, and often not institutionalized, are a new circumstance. This means that the relation of Christ to non-Christian religions, as well as to these personally constructed spiritualities, is no longer a matter of theorizing from a safe distance but rather a matter of daily encounter in neighborhoods, in schools, at work, at the gas station, and at the supermarket. And what will prove to be even more momentous in the evangelical world than its engagement with the other religions, I believe, will be whether it is able to distinguish what it has to offer from the emergence of these forms of spirituality. Therapeutic spiritualities that are non-religious begin to look quite like evangelical spirituality that is therapeutic and non-doctrinal.

These two developments—*the emergence of the postmodern ethos* and *the growing religious and spiritual diversity*—are by no means parallel or even complementary, but they are unmistakably defining American culture in a significantly new way. And they are defining the context within which the church must live out its life. Already there are some signs that this engagement with culture is not exactly going the church's way. It was certainly noticeable that, following September 11, the church was mostly unable to offer any public reading on the tragedy that did anything more than commiserate with those who had lost loved ones. There was virtually no Christian interpretation, no wrestling with the meaning of evil, little thought about the cross where Christians contend its back was broken.

### Christ and Context

In 1984, I wrote a traditional Christology entitled *The Person of Christ: A Biblical and Historical Analysis of the Incarnation.*[2] This volume was part of a series in which each of the authors was asked to follow the same format: about one-third was to be devoted to the biblical materials, one-third to historical developments, and the remaining third to a discussion of three or four contemporary thinkers. This is the sort of foundational work which needs to be done in developing a Christology. The questions that such an account seeks to address are almost always those that are *internal* to the church or academia. This is entirely appropriate. These issues, such as how the person of Christ is spoken of by the different authors of the New Testament, how these lines of thought were taken up in the early church, how they were debated in the Middle Ages and Reformation, and how they have been formulated by recent scholars, are central and necessary considerations in a Christology. However, it has become increasingly clear to me that while these internal issues are of vital importance, they are not the only issues that should be engaging the church. They are the indispensable, foundational questions, but they do not comprise everything that the church should be thinking about with respect to the person of Christ. There are also issues that are *external* in nature that should accompany this foundational work. These are concerned with how a Christology faces off against, how it engages, its own cultural context.

That being the case, the volume that I wrote earlier, in 1984, remains foundational to this present analysis. Nothing has changed in the conclusions I reached then, nor should they, for they echo the biblical testimony. What has changed is a growing concern on my part to be able to say more exactly how Christ, in whom divine majesty and

---

[2]David F. Wells, *The Person of Christ: A Biblical and Historical Analysis of the Incarnation* (Wheaton, IL: Crossway Books, 1984).

human frailty are joined in one person, is to be heard and preached in a postmodern, multiethnic, multireligious society. Indeed, not to proceed in this endeavor would be an unhappy outcome because theology, if it is true to its own nature, must be missiological[3] in its intent. Its task is not only to understand the nature of biblical truth but also to ask how that truth addresses the issues of the day. Churches today who send out missionaries to other parts of the world would be considered greatly mistaken if they instructed those missionaries to depend only on the Word of God and not to attempt to understand the people to whom they have been sent to minister.

The history of the church shows that in every generation there are cultural challenges. The two motifs that are now transforming culture—the emergence of the postmodern ethos and the new, growing tidal wave of religious pluralism—are deep and powerful currents that are flowing through the nation. But they are not peculiar to America. In fact, Europe appears to be well ahead of the United States in its experience of postmodernity, and it also appears to be caught in more painful perplexity about immigration and its consequences. Yet there is nothing in the modern world that is a match for the power of God and nothing in modern culture which diminishes our understanding of the supremacy of Christ. From this vantage point, I have attempted in the following pages to think about the message of Christ from within the postmodern world I have spent time describing. In the first section I take up the theme of spirituality, which really speaks with the soul of postmodernity, and in the second I address how postmodern unbelief is expressing itself in the language of the meaninglessness of life.

## Christ in a Spiritual World

We begin our exploration with the emergence of a new kind of spiritual person: one who is on a spiritual quest but often pursuing this in oppo-

---

[3]I have developed the missiological nature of theology in several essays which deal with its methodology: "The Nature and Function of Theology," in *The Use of the Bible in Theology*, ed. Robert K. Johnston (Atlanta: John Knox Press, 1983), 175–99; "An American Evangelical Theology: The Painful Transition from *Theoria* to *Praxis*," in *Evangelicalism and Modern America*, ed. George Marsden (Grand Rapids, MI: Eerdmans, 1984), 83–93; "Word and World: Biblical Authority and the Quandary of Modernity," in *Evangelical Affirmations*, ed. Kenneth S. Kantzer and Carl F. Henry (Grand Rapids, MI: Zondervan, 1990), 153–76; "The Theologian's Craft," in *Doing Theology in Today's World: Essays in Honor of Kenneth S. Kantzer*, ed. John Woodbridge and Thomas McComiskey (Grand Rapids, MI: Zondervan, 1991), 171–94; and "The Theology of Preaching," in *God's Living Word: Essays in Preaching*, ed. Theodore Stylianopoulis (Brookline, MA: Holy Cross Press, 1983), 57–70.

sition to what is religious. That, however, may be stating the matter a little too starkly, for it suggests that religions are being understood in terms of what they actually assert. In reality, religions tend to blur in the postmodern mind and become undifferentiated from each other. That is the almost inevitable outcome of our pluralism. When religions become aware of each other in the postmodern world, they typically either lose their sharp edges or are at least seen as having done so. It is as predictable as it is desultory that 44 percent of Americans think that "the Bible, the Koran and the Book of Mormon are different expressions of the same spiritual truths."[4] Yet it remains the case that this spirituality sees itself as other than what is religious, be this religion that is insistently doctrinal or religion that has become blurred by its passage through the postmodern spirit. Such spirituality threatens to rumble through evangelical faith in a way more detrimental to it than any Christian engagement with non-Christian religions. In this section, then, I need to accomplish three things: first, I need to provide some description of this new spiritual search; second, I will explore the parallels that exist between this new quest and what the church has faced before, especially in the patristic period; and, third, I need to outline what a biblical response to this search looks like.

## The New Spiritual Yearning

These new spiritualities are now taking their place alongside some older ones, spiritualities that are often defined over against religion but nevertheless are not averse to incorporating religious ideas. Individuals and groups who have thus turned to things spiritual have, since the 1960s, had assorted goals, some of which also overlap. For some, the aim has been that of finding peace of mind or inner transformation; in its Eastern configuration, the goal has been achieving a different kind of consciousness; in its shallowest and most banal form, it is about self-awareness, self-esteem, and self-actualization, achievements which may come in a purely secular form or as a part of spiritual self-discovery; and for contemporary gnostics, the hope is empowerment—not in the ways we encounter in gender politics, which are frequently fueled by resentment, but in the sense of connecting with a power deep within the self.

---

[4]George Barna, "Americans Draw Theological Beliefs from Diverse Points of View," October 8, 2002. Available online at http://www.barna.org.

When the Enlightenment mindset dominated American culture, those who said that they looked within themselves for answers were, in all likelihood, secularists and humanists of one kind or another. In the postmodern moment in which we are living, however, those who look within themselves are not necessarily divorcing themselves from the sacred. On the contrary, many are actually believers in the sacred, which they are pursuing within themselves. They are not seeking the God of the Christian religion, who is transcendent, who speaks to life from outside of it and entered it through the Incarnation, whose Word is absolute and enduring, and whose moral character defines the difference between Good and Evil forever. Rather, it is the god within, the god who is found within the self and in whom the self is rooted. This is, for the most part, a simple perception, and as found spread throughout American society it comes with few pretensions to having great intellectual depth. Yet that is not always the case. Mircea Eliade, for example, has spoken of the "irruption of the sacred"[5] within life and of the complex ways in which myths and dreams are rooted in the manifestations of the divine within. It is the same belief, then, that comes sometimes in homely ways and sometimes wrapped in complexity—and yet this inward presence invariably proves to be elusive, and so the search is always unfinished. In this searching, it is hoped, there will be found the balm of therapeutic comfort, the suggestion of meaning and of connectedness to something larger.

Such searchers would include many of the 56 percent among Americans who say that in life's crises they look within themselves for answers rather than to an outside power like the Christian God.[6] They are in search of a new *consciousness*. If they speak of *transformation*, as so many do, it is in terms of their own human potential, the innate sources of personal renewal that lie deep within. If they speak of their own *intuitions*, as they often do, it is with the sense of having onboard a navigational system that enables them to find their place in reality. Or, perhaps more correctly, it allows them to find a better place in reality. And if they speak of a *connectedness* for which they yearn, it is in the blurry sense that somehow the human and divine are no longer disengaged from each other but, rather, are implicated in each other.

---

[5]Mircea Eliade, *Myths, Dreams, and Mysteries: The Encounter Between Contemporary Faiths and Archaic Realities*, trans. Philip Mairet (New York: Harper, 1960), 15.
[6]Barna, "Americans Draw Theological Beliefs from Diverse Points of View."

An outside God, such as we find in biblical faith, is comprehensible because he is self-defined in his revelation; the inside god is not. The inside god is merged into the psychological texture of the seeker and found spread within the vagaries of the self. The outside God stands over against those who would know him; the inside one emerges within their consciousness and is a part of them. Religions have their schools of thought and their interpreters, and always the debate is over who most truly understands the religion. Spirituality, in the contemporary sense, spawns no such debate because it makes no truth claims and seeks no universal significance. It lives out its life within the confines of private experience. "Truth" is private, not public; it is for the individual, not for the universe. Here is American individualism coupled with some new assumptions about God that are being glossed off with infatuations about pop therapy, uniting to produce varieties of spirituality as numerous as those who think of themselves as spiritual.

The spiritual journey in this contemporary sense does not begin with what has been given by God or with what does not change. Rather, it begins with the self. It begins in the soil of human autonomy and it gives to the self the authority to decide what to believe, from what sources to draw knowledge and inspiration, and how to test the viability of what is believed. The result is that this kind of spirituality is inevitably experimental and even libertarian. Its validation comes through the psychological or therapeutic benefits that are derived. Mixing and matching, discarding or reappropriating ideas in an endless process of searching and experimenting, is what this spirituality is about.

To say, as Harold Bloom does, that this spirituality is "gnosticism," and that gnosticism is the "American religion,"[7] is, from a historical and conceptual point of view, too heavy-handed to be helpful. Nevertheless, Bloom's case could be better made along slightly different, and more nuanced, lines.

The point of connection with the past is not so much gnosticism

---

[7]This "religion," Bloom argues, resolves itself into a spiritual quest in which the self is both subject and object of the search. His argument is that this quest underlies much overt religion that on the surface expresses itself doctrinally and in very different ways—Roman Catholic, Mormon, Seventh-Day Adventist, and Southern Baptist. See his *The American Religion: The Emergence of the Post-Christian Nation* (New York: Simon and Schuster, 1992). As a part of his argument he claims that America is gnostic without knowing it: *Omens of Millennium: The Gnosis of Angels, Dreams, and Resurrection* (New York: Riverhead Books, 1996), 183.

but, rather, a primal spirituality which, in the early period of the church's life, came into expression as gnosticism. The theories of gnosticism were defeated and soon forgotten. However, the spirituality that they were seeking to explain is the point of connection with the past. It is this spirituality rooted in the self that assumes the liberty either to oppose or appropriate external religious forms but is resolute in its opposition to having to submit to external religious authority. It is in these ways that we are also seeing the convergence between this primal spirituality and a resurgent paganism.

When Christian faith encountered this spirituality in the early centuries, Anders Nygren declares, it had arrived at "its hour of destiny."[8] This was so because this spirituality was, in its outworkings, its beliefs, and its view of life, the polar opposite of what we find in Christian faith. It was an opponent. And the besetting temptation that the Church would encounter, sometimes in fierce ways and at other times in more subtle ways, was to wonder if it could lessen the fierceness of the competition by incorporating in itself elements of this pagan way of looking at the spiritual life. These two spiritualities, Christian and pagan, Nygren contrasts in the language of two very different kinds of love, *Agape* and *Eros*. From this time forth, and coming right down into the contemporary moment, the struggle is going to be how Agape is going to preserve itself from the persistent intrusions of Eros.

The opening salvos were, of course, fired in the conflict in the early church over gnosticism; today, they are being fired by the new spirituality. Although the gnosticism of the patristic period was only one particular expression of Eros, it is, nevertheless, worth revisiting because of its parallels with postmodern spirituality.

## An Ancient Spirituality

Ancient gnosticism, like the contemporary spiritual search, was a very diverse movement, and it is hard to provide a succinct definition of it. Irenaeus's survey shows how variegated the gnostic world was,[9] though as a set of movements, as distinct from intellectual influences, none predated the Christian faith despite Bultmann's claim.[10] The diversity of these movements arose from the fact that the influences behind them

---

[8]Anders Nygren, *Agape and Eros*, trans. Philip Watson (London: S.P.C.K., 1953), 30.
[9]Irenaeus, *Against Heresies*, I, i, 1–I, vii, 5; I, xi, 1–I, xx, 3; I, xxiii, 1–I, xxxi, 4.
[10]See Edwin M. Yamauchi, "Some Alleged Evidences for Pre-Christian Gnosticism," in *New*

were different: some had their roots in Eastern theosophy, others Greek philosophical speculation, and still others mystical Judaism. These sources produced some very different outcomes among the competing schools of gnostic thought which took root in Egypt and Syria, and along the eastern coast of the Mediterranean. Over time, after gnosticism had become a set of movements that paralleled the church, it changed shape and in mid-career began to appropriate Christian ideas and attempted to incorporate Christian faith into its larger framework. In its final development it came right into the church, and, in thinkers like Valentinus, Marcion, and Basilides, it passed itself off as being an authentic expression of Christianity, thereby confounding definition even further.

Gnosticism proved to be an especially nettlesome matter in the early church, not because the novelty of its ideas swept people off their feet, but because its ideas, in some important respects, already pervaded that ancient world. They seemed normal, natural, and familiar. There had already been a long history of thought on some of its key elements in the East. It is not clear how Eastern thought reached Greece, but classical Greek philosophy sometimes followed some of the important paths blazed in the East, and these ideas had already permeated the world in which the church had been planted.

Here, too, is an echo of our own times. The combination of a modernized social fabric and the Enlightenment ideology that took root in it until relatively recently produced the *autonomous self*. This is the self that is not subject to outside authority and into which all reality has been contracted. The result is a radicalized individualism with a deeply privatized outlook and a mood that is insistently therapeutic. All of this has produced soil throughout society that positively invites the new spirituality. It seems normal and natural. That is why it is as difficult for the church to contest today as was gnosticism in the early centuries.

Classical Greek philosophy, like Eastern thought, depreciated the natural world and pondered the soul's alienation from it. And like the philosophies of the East, Greek thought typically came to think of the soul as being not a divine creation but a shard that had fallen away

---

*Dimensions in New Testament Study*, ed. Richard N. Longenecker and Merrill C. Tenney (Grand Rapids, MI: Zondervan, 1974), 46–70.

from the All or Absolute and was now found in a human body. Its sense of alienation from the world came from the individuality by which it was now afflicted, individuality which expressed itself in thought and consciousness.

Greek philosophy struggled with how to relate the divine, which is remote and removed from life, with the soul and its struggles within the body. And that was where the Gnostics pushed the argument forward one or two steps. At the heart of their spiritual quest was a search for the answer to evil. Wherever they looked, whether to the firmament above or to the bodies in which their consciousness resided, what they saw was a monumentally failed work, a creation that was awry, corrupt, nefarious, and dark. All gnostic systems of thought, as a result, were philosophically dualistic or semi-dualistic, positing that what had been made had been made by an enemy of human beings. There were differences of opinion as to how to work this all out, but typically it led to the notion that either there were two ultimate principles in the universe, one good and one bad, the latter being responsible for the creation, or there was only one ultimate principle from which a series of emanations and spirits had proceeded, one of whom was eventually so far from the source of good as to be able to bring about this wretched creation. What the various gnostic teachers sought to do was to bring understanding about the human plight, to inculcate insight about the very nature of things, and, most importantly, to get people in touch with their spiritual natures. Only then could there be liberation from the clutches of what was evil.

So what is the nature of this insight that held the key to self-liberation for these ancient gnostics? It is, of course, "knowledge." This was not really intellectual knowledge, though it was often accompanied by complex philosophical speculation. It was more of a private insight, an internal revelation, a spiritual perception, one given from within. It was not so much knowledge of God that was sought, for he was perceived to be ineffable, distant, removed, and unattainable. He is, as Valentinus said, "that Incomprehensible, Inconceivable (One), who is superior to all thought" and who, in fact, is beyond the range of all human thought.[11] They were far more interested in pursuing what was inside in the self.

---

[11] Valentinus, *Evangelium Veritatis*, IX, 5.

This pursuit of the knowledge of the self rested upon a double assumption. The first was, in modern terms, that *theology is nothing other than anthropology*. "For gnostics," Elaine Pagels explains, "exploring the *psyche* became explicitly what it is for many people today implicitly—a religious quest," not least because gnostics believed a fragment of divinity was lodged somewhere in their interior world.[12] What they also assumed is that *people stumble, suffer, and make mistakes not because of sin but because of ignorance*. It was, of course, to remedy this ignorance that, in the Christian phase of gnosticism, the Son was seen as bringing "knowledge" of the Father—yet this was a far cry from knowledge as it is construed biblically. Thus it is that both ancient gnostics and those postmoderns who place such value on psychotherapeutic techniques do so because above all other things they value "the self-knowledge," Pagels notes, "which is insight."[13] And this self-knowledge functions in a revelatory way which is only possible, we need to note, because of the lost understanding of sin. It is ignorance, ignorance of ourselves and especially of our spiritual nature, gnostics believed, that is the key to our ignorance of the nature of things, and of the grip that evil exercises invisibly on all things created and on ourselves not least. And it is the self that, in this situation, reveals its own connections into what is divine.

One of the chief contentions of the gnostics in their polemics against the church was that "knowledge," in their understanding of it, is superior to "faith." They might as well have said that they were pursuing spirituality, rather than religion, for that is what they meant. They were opposed to a doctrinally shaped and governed Christianity. They were instead pursuing enlightenment through the self, for this kind of understanding, they believed, was itself revelatory. This did not mean that they always eschewed organized religion, for some gnostics entered the churches and suggested that they were the most authentic realization of Christian faith. However, for them the church was never more than a means toward the end of their pursuit of psychic knowledge, a circumstance being played out again in church after church in the postmodern world where consumer habits have hooked up with a therapeutic orientation that now is subjugating religion to spirituality and spirituality to private choice.

---

[12]Elaine Pagels, *The Gnostic Gospels* (New York: Random House, 1979), 123.
[13]Ibid., 124.

In one very important respect, however, gnosticism was the antithesis of another of the church's rivals, paganism. Paganism was about nature; gnosticism was in flight from nature. Gnostics saw themselves as caught in a creation that is flawed, dark, and ominous, whose rhythms bring no connections with anything divine, and whose God is far away, alienated, aloof, and incommunicative. In this respect, they were far removed from the pantheism that was at the heart of paganism. Speaking for gnostics of all times, Bloom argues that the creator God is a "bungler" who "botched" the creation and precipitated the fall.[14] This creation offers no home for the human being because, he argues, originally "the deepest self was not part of creation" but was part of the "fullness of God" to which it yearns to return. This yearning, this homesickness, is what often passes as depression, he suggests. And yet, despite this significant difference, there is also an important point of convergence. "God," Bloom tells us, "is at once deep within the self and also estranged, infinitely far off, beyond our cosmos."[15] Here lies the point of connection with paganism: not in the worship of nature (cf. Rom. 1:18–24), but in the access to the sacred that is sought through the self, this "deepest self," which experiences itself as being adrift from life, as not being able to fit in with life, and as offering an exit from the oppressive complexities and manifold pains of this "botched" creation into what is eternal.

## A Christian Response

### Clash of Worldviews

It seems rather clear, then, that our contemporary spirituality is in continuity with some of the different aspects of what has preceded it. In some of its expressions it has more in common with paganism; in others it is more like gnosticism. New Age, for example, what Bloom mocks as "an endlessly entertaining saturnalia of ill-defined yearnings . . . suspended about halfway between feeling good and good feeling" and "a vacuity not to be believed," has affinities that are more obviously pagan, but this wider spirituality, as we have seen, finds significant parallels in gnosticism.

Seeing how this spiritual search is both contemporary and ancient

---

[14]Bloom, *Omens of Millennium*, 27.
[15]Ibid., 30.

is really the key to understanding how to think about it from a Christian point of view. To put the matter succinctly: those who see only the contemporaneity of this spirituality—and who, typically, yearn to be seen as being contemporary—usually make tactical maneuvers to win a hearing for their Christian views; those who see its underlying worldview will not. Inevitably, those enamored by its contemporaneity will find that with each new tactical repositioning they are drawn irresistibly into the vortex of what they think is merely contemporary but what, in actual fact, also has the power to contaminate their faith. What they should be doing is thinking strategically, not tactically. To do so is to begin to see how ancient this spirituality actually is and to understand that beneath many contemporary styles, tastes, and habits there are also encountered rival *worldviews*. When rival worldviews are in play, it is not adaptation that is called for but confrontation: confrontation not of a behavioral kind which is lacking in love but of a cognitive kind which holds forth "the truth in love" (Eph. 4:15). This is one of the great lessons learned from the early church. Despite the few who wobbled, most of its leaders maintained with an admirable tenacity the alternative view of life which was rooted in the apostolic teaching. They did not allow love to blur truth or to substitute for it but sought to live by both truth and love.

A worldview is a framework for understanding the world. It is the perspective through which we see what is ultimate, what is real, what our experience means, and what our place is in the cosmos. It is in these ways that we might speak of postmodernity as having a worldview despite the denials of its advocates and practitioners. What they are denying is having an *Enlightenment* worldview, one which is rationally structured and, from their perspective, one that is pretentious because it is claiming to know much too much. Everyone, however, has a worldview, even if it is one which posits no meaning and even if it is one that is entirely private and true only for the person who holds it.

We must go further, however. It is not just any worldview that we encounter in the postmodern world, but one that increasingly resembles the old paganisms. It is one that is antithetical to that which biblical faith requires. It is this transformation of our world, this emerging worldview, that has passed largely unnoticed. That, at least, is the most charitable conclusion that one can draw. For while the evangelical church is aware of such things as the fight for gay and lesbian rights, hears about the eco-feminists, knows about pornography, has a sense that moral absolutes are evaporating like the morning mist, knows that truth of an ultimate kind has been dislodged from life, it apparently does not perceive that in these and many other ways a new worldview is becoming ensconced in the culture. If it did, it surely would not be embracing with enthusiasm as many aspects of this postmodern mindset as it is or be so willing to make concessions to postmodern habits of mind.[16]

This casual embrace of what is postmodern has increasingly led to an embrace of its spiritual yearning without noticing that this embrace carries within it the seeds of destruction for evangelical faith. The contrast between biblical faith and this contemporary spirituality is that between two entirely different ways of looking at life and at God. Nygren, as noted earlier, used the Greek words for two different kinds of love, *Eros* and *Agape*, to characterize these worldviews, and his elucidation is still helpful. In the one worldview, which he calls Eros, it is the self which is in the center. Eros, Nygren says, has at its heart a kind of want, longing, or yearning.[17] It is this fact, of course, which has always put the church in something of a conundrum. Is this yearning a natural preparation for the gospel, human nature crying out in its emptiness, calling out to be filled with something else? It was this thought that led Clement of Alexandria in the early church to speak of the "true Christian gnostic" as if gnosticism's yearning for what was spiritual reached its fulfillment in Christian faith. Yet if this yearning

---

[16]The dichotomy that postmodern epistemology wants to force is one between knowing everything exhaustively and knowing nothing certainly at all. And since it would be arrogant in the extreme to claim to know what God alone knows, the only other option, it seems, is to accept the fact that our knowledge is so socially conditioned, so determined by our own inability to escape our own relativity, that we are left with no certain knowledge of reality at all. This is the epistemological position accepted by Richard Middleton and Brian Walsh. All attempts at "getting reality" right, they say, have proved to be failures, and Christians should concede as much. See their *Truth Is Stranger Than It Used to Be* (Downers Grove, IL: InterVarsity Press, 1995). From a slightly different angle, Brian McLaren has adopted as a positive, even God-directed, development the disjunction between spirituality and religion. The religion in question for him is still evangelical, but the disjuncture he promotes leaves behind a faith that is suspicious of reason, resistant to formulated beliefs, and allergic to structures within which faith is practiced, and, of course, it is dismissive of worldviews. Unless these attitudes are allowed to reshape the way Christianity is lived out, he believes, it is doomed to die. Here, indeed, is the old liberal fear of becoming outdated coupled with the postmodern infatuation with spirituality in its divorce from religion. See his *A New Kind of Christian: A Tale of Two Friends on a Spiritual Journey* (San Francisco: Jossey-Bass, 2001). In the cases of Middleton, Walsh, and McLaren, then, the adoption of a postmodern worldview is not inadvertent at all but knowing and deliberate.

[17]Nygren, *Agape and Eros*, 210.

is a preparation, it is one that stands in need of serious purging, for it carries within itself an understanding about God and salvation that is diametrically opposed to what we have in biblical faith. In this sense, it is less a preparation and more of a wrong turn. Why is this so?

The movement of Eros spirituality is upward. Its essence, its drive, is the sinner finding God. The movement of Agape, by contrast, is downward. It is all about God finding the sinner. Eros spirituality is the kind of spirituality that arises from human nature, and it builds on the presumption that it can forge its own salvation. Agape arises in God, was incarnate in Christ, and reaches us through the work of the Holy Spirit opening lives to receive the gospel of Christ's saving death. In this understanding, salvation is given and never forged or manufactured. Eros is the projection of the human spirit into eternity, the immortalizing of its own impulses. Agape is the intrusion of eternity into the fabric of life, coming not from below, but from above. Eros is human love. Agape is divine love. Human love of this kind, because it has need and want at its center, because it is always wanting to have its needs and wants satisfied, will always seek to control the object of its desires. That is why in these new spiritualities it is the spiritual person who makes up his or her beliefs and practices, mixing and matching and experimenting to see what works best and assuming the prerogative to discard at will. The sacred is therefore loved for what can be had from loving it. The sacred is pursued because it has value to the pursuer, and that value is measured in terms of the therapeutic payoff. There is, therefore, always a profit-and-loss mentality to these spiritualities.

### Sin's Disappearance

The premise beneath all of these spiritualities is that sin has not intruded upon the relation between the sacred and human nature, that human nature itself offers access—indeed, we assume, unblemished access—to God, that human nature itself mediates the divine. Gone are the days when people understood that an avalanche has fallen between God and human beings, that human nature retains its shape as made in the image of God but has lost its relationship to God and stands in pained alienation from him.

It is no small anomaly that we have arrived at this point. How can we be so knowledgeable about evil in the world and so innocent about sin in ourselves? Is it not strange that we who see so much tragedy through television, who are so knowledgeable of the darkness in our world, who pride ourselves on being able to stare with clear eyes and no denials at what is messy, untidy, ugly, and painful, are also those who know so little about sin in ourselves?

The reason, of course, is that we have lost the moral world in which sin is alone understood.[18] The religious authorities who once gave us rules for life and who gave us the metaphysical world in which those rules found their grounding have all faded in our moral imagination. Today, we are more alone in this world than any previous generation.[19]

The consequence is that we have come to believe that the self retains its access to the sacred, an access not ruptured by sin. In 2002, a national survey by Barna turned up the astounding discovery that despite all of the difficulties that modernized life has created, despite its rapaciousness, greed, and violence, 74 percent of those surveyed rejected the idea of original sin and 52 percent of evangelicals concurred. These were the percentages of respondents who agreed with the statement that "when people are born they are neither good nor evil—they make a choice between the two as they mature."[20] Here is raw American individualism and the heresy of Pelagianism, which asserts that people are born innocent of sin, that sin is a set of bad practices that is caught later on in life rather like a disease. It is our lost moral compass that produces this fallacious understanding of human nature, and it is this fallacious understanding that fuels and drives Eros spirituality.

### Confrontation, Not Tactics

As previously noted, church talk about "reaching" the culture turns, almost inevitably, into a discussion about tactics and methodology, not about worldviews. It is only about tactics and not about strategy. It is about seduction and not about truth, about success and not about confrontation. However, without *strategy*, the tactics inevitably fail; without *truth*, all of the arts of seduction that the churches are prac-

---

[18]See Andrew Delbanco, *The Death of Satan: How Americans Have Lost the Sense of Evil* (New York: Farrar, Straus and Giroux, 1995).

[19]James Patterson and Peter Kim, *The Day America Told the Truth: What People Really Believe about Everything That Matters* (New York: Prentice Hall, 1991), 27.

[20]Barna, "Americans Draw Theological Beliefs from Diverse Points of View."

ticing sooner or later are seen for what they are—an empty charade; and because the emerging worldview is not being engaged, the church has little it can really say. Indeed, one has to ask how much it actually wants to say. Biblical truth contradicts this cultural spirituality, and that contradiction is hard to bear. Biblical truth displaces it, refuses to allow its operating assumptions, declares to it its bankruptcy. Is the evangelical church faithful enough to explode the worldview of this new spiritual search? Is it brave enough to contradict what has wide cultural approval? The final verdict may not be in, but it seems quite apparent that while the culture is burning, the evangelical church is fiddling precisely because it has decided it must be so like the culture to be successful.

## Christ in a Meaningless World

Postmoderns are remarkably nonchalant about the meaninglessness that they experience in life. Reading the works of an earlier generation of writers, existentialist authors like Jean-Paul Sartre and Albert Camus, one almost develops a sense of vertigo, the kind of apprehension that one gets when standing too near the edge of a terrifying precipice, so bleak, empty, and life-threatening was their vision. That sense, however, has now completely gone. Postmoderns live on the surface, not in the depths, and theirs is a despair to be tossed off lightly and which might even be alleviated by nothing more serious than a sitcom. There are today few of the convulsions that once happened in the depths of the human spirit. These are different responses to the same sense of meaninglessness, which is one of the threads that weaves its way from the modern past into the postmodern present. What changes is simply how those afflicted with the drift and emptiness of postmodern life cope with it. In this section, then, I first need to explore this theme; second, I want to frame this meaninglessness theologically; and third, I need to think about how life's meaninglessness is addressed by Christ's gospel.

## The Culture of Nothingness

"The first half of the twentieth century," writes Daniel Boorstin, was a time of "triumphal and accelerating science," and yet it "produced a literature of bewilderment without precedent in our history."[21] At the time, this development in the modern world may have seemed strange. In the very moment of social conquest—when science and technology were promising to rewrite the script of life, to eliminate more and more diseases, to make life more bearable, to fill it with more goods—at that very moment the human spirit was sagging beneath the burden of emptiness, apparently ungrateful for all of this modern bounty.

In retrospect, however, it is not so strange. This was the moment when the Enlightenment world, which had promised so much, was showing the first symptoms of the postmodern ethos of the West, of that curdling of the soul that would leave the human being replete with goods, smothered in plenty, but totally alone in the cosmos, isolated, alienated, enclosed within itself, and bewildered. The conquest of the world, the triumph of technology, and the omnipresence of shopping malls—our temples to consumption—are not the tools by which the human spirit can be repaired. Of that there should be no doubt now, for if affluence, and the bright, shiny world in which it arises, could be the solvent of all human maladies that lie submerged beneath the surface of life, then this *anomie*, this bewilderment of soul, would long since have been banished. The truth, in fact, is that the conquest of our external world seems to be in inverse relation to the conquest of our inner world. The more we triumph in the one, the less we seem able to hold together in the other.[22]

The appearance of this despairing mood earlier on is, of course, associated with a wide swath of writers, but at mid-century it came to the fore not only in Sartre and Camus, but also in writers such as Eugene Ionesco, Samuel Beckett, Harold Pinter, Martin Heidegger, and others, not all of whom were existentialists. In their different ways they were all reflecting the empty world they inhabited. It was empty because, on the intellectual side in the West, finding any ultimate grounding for things has become an increasingly precarious undertaking. This nihil-

[21]Daniel J. Boorstin, *The Seekers: The Story of Man's Continuing Quest to Understand His World* (New York: Random House, 1998), 228.

[22]This is the "American Paradox." The paradox, says David Myers, is that we "are better paid, better fed, better housed, better educated, and healthier than ever before, and with more human rights, faster communication, and more convenient transportation than we have ever known." Alongside all of this largesse, however, are the signs of life in pain and travail. Since 1960, the divorce rate has doubled, teen suicide has tripled, violent crime quadrupled, the number in prison has quintupled, illegitimate children sextupled, and the number of those cohabitating has increased sevenfold. David G. Myers, *The American Paradox: Spiritual Hunger in an Age of Plenty* (New Haven, CT: Yale University Press, 2000), 5.

ism, whether philosophically conceived or merely assumed amidst the trappings and doings of Western influence, has moved out along different avenues depending upon which of several aspects is emphasized. At root, however, it operates by denying that objective ground exists for believing that anything is true or right—or simply by assuming none does. It denies that anything can be ultimate because ultimately nothing is there. There is no hub to hold the spokes; or if there is, we are unable to get our cognitive sights on it. This sometimes takes the form that one can know nothing certainly, that what is true and what is not cannot be distinguished, and that all knowledge is merely an internal construct in which the outcomes are, as a result, always provisional; still others press the attack on reality itself, arguing that in the end nothing is, in fact, real. And in the absence of any reality in which truth can be grounded, all that remains in life is power, as Nietzsche saw so clearly. If there is no ultimate reality before which we are accountable for what we think, say, and do, then there are no restraints upon the exercise of power, upon the imposition of our will on others, either at a personal level or by corporations, ethnic groups, or the state.

In America, the disintegration of the self and the disintegration of its world are not commonly expressed in the dark language of this earlier literature, though there are exceptions to this in some of the rock music from the 1970s onward which is full not only of obscenities but of violence, hatred, and fear in a world turned empty. More typically, though, when this bewilderment spilled out into the wider culture in America, it lost its edge. In this earlier literature, there were a sharpness, a painful aching loss, an unbearable emptiness, a disorientation of being, but when this sense of dislocation from life became domesticated in the wider culture it also became much tamer. It lost its acuteness. By the 1990s, when we encounter the television series *Seinfeld*, for example, this sense of internal loss and disorientation had been turned into a brilliantly acted but completely banal sitcom. *Seinfeld*, Thomas Hibbs writes, was "a show about the comical consequences of life in a world void of ultimate significance or fundamental meaning." This show, he adds, was "by its own account, a show about nothing."[23] The darkness of soul had lifted, though not its emptiness. Now we were no

---

[23]Thomas S. Hibbs, *Shows about Nothing: Nihilism in Popular Culture from* The Exorcist *to* Seinfeld (Dallas: Spence, 1999), 22.

longer serious enough to do anything but smirk. The journey into the postmodern world, from the writers of the literature of bewilderment into television shows like this, is one from darkness in the depths to mockery on the surface, from suicide to shallow snickers. The Void is constant; how we live with it is where the differences arise.

Such loss of any grounding for meaning also eats away at hope. Viktor Frankl, a psychiatrist who was taken off to the Nazi death camps during the Second World War, has written with poignant clarity about those who survived and those who did not and in so doing illustrates this point. In the camps, the prisoners were stripped of every semblance of dignity and identity and were under constant threat of death. He wrote about the deadening of emotion that happened as a result, the apathy that so often took hold, and the protective shell of insensitivity in which they took refuge because they had to see so many unspeakable horrors. He also noted that under threat of constant beatings, insults, and degradation, prisoners had only their inner lives left, and here they could "find a refuge from the emptiness, desolation and spiritual poverty" of their existence.[24] Every strategy was used to stay alive. One of these was to rob the present of its power of destruction by dwelling in the past, by letting the imagination return to past events, to revisit other people, and by doing so to enter a different world. However, although the past offered some fleeting respite, it was the future that held out the hope for survival. Those who could see no future for themselves simply gave up. They were doomed. "With this loss of belief in the future," he wrote, such a person "also lost his spiritual hold." The prisoner would typically refuse one day to get dressed. Blows, curses, threats, and whippings were to no avail. The prisoner had given up. For such a prisoner, meaning had died because there was nothing left for which to survive.[25]

What is so striking is the comparison that naturally arises between these prisoners who had been stripped of every remnant of dignity and reduced to disposable refuse, and those in the postmodern West who likewise have lost their hold on meaning but for precisely the opposite reason. They have not been deprived of everything, nor have they been treated brutally. On the contrary, they have everything; they live with

---

[24]Viktor E. Frankl, *Man's Search for Meaning: An Introduction to Logotherapy*, trans. Ilse Lasch (New York: Simon and Schuster, 1959), 38.
[25]Ibid., 74.

unprecedented convenience and freedom, but the future in a world without meaning is as impotent to summon up hope and direction as was that of the prisoners who gave up in the camps. The difference, however, is that these postmoderns, unlike the prisoners, have ways of offsetting this inner corrosion. Luxury and plenty, entertainment and recreation, sex and drugs, become the ways of creating surrogate meaning or momentary distraction, or at least some numbness. It is surrogate meaning and distraction to conceal the inner blankness, the depletion of self, so that its aches can be forgotten.

### This Side of the Sun

Seen within a theological framework, the question of contemporary meaninglessness is one, I would argue, that has two sides to it, sociological and soteriological. Biblically speaking, meaninglessness is primarily *soteriological* in nature and only secondarily sociological; as it is experienced by people, its soteriological nature is often not comprehended. If anything is comprehended at all, it is only what is sociological, and that might well be misconstrued.

Today, postmodern culture inclines people to see the world as if it had been stripped of its structures of meaning, of its morality, of any viable worldview that is universal, and it collapses all of reality into the self. It eats away at every vestige of meaning for which people grasp. In these ways, it is one of the forms in which the biblical understanding of "the world" takes shape in the West. It therefore adds weight, or gives further reality, to what is soteriological, to that emptiness of human experience which is the outcome to alienation from God and which is the present consequence of his wrath. It is the consequence of being relationally severed from him. And that is registered in the twilight knowledge of God that still persists in human consciousness, leaving people "without excuse," but the relational disjuncture is so substantial and complete as to leave them always disoriented, always caught in the coils of painful futility.

Nowhere is this better illuminated than in the book of Ecclesiastes. Its opening salvo is the author's refrain, "vanity of vanities" (1:2), which recurs some thirty-one times in the book. How utterly transitory, empty, and meaningless is life! It is nothing but the pursuit of the wind. That is the word of the Preacher, considered by many to have been Israel's King Solomon. And what he recounts is his tortured search for some contentment, some respite from, even some escape from, the relentlessly empty world he came to inhabit "under the sun."

It is useless, Solomon said, to seek for wisdom that unlocks the meaning of life, for in his search he had found only futility (Eccl. 1:17). The human being is afflicted by the longing for knowledge but thwarted in its pursuit. What we see is but the passing, fading surface, and what lies behind it is lost in obscurity. This initial search for wisdom, then, brought Solomon no peace, no inner quietude, but rather restlessness and sorrow. Nor did he find any relief in party-making, revelry, and pleasure-seeking. All of this turned out to be hollow and empty as well (2:1–2). The emptiness within could not be assuaged by ceaseless activity, or by work, or wealth (2:4–11; 4:7–12). Work brings no unmitigated pleasure but only care and carping (4:4–6). "So I turned about and gave my heart up to despair over all the toil of my labors under the sun"—the rewards of which would, in any case, be inherited by another (2:20). Thus did the Preacher demolish every attempt at finding meaning "under the sun" in a fallen world. For him, it was not possible for Eros to reach into the infinite and find meaning.

Nor was Solomon alone in expressing this outlook. A number of the sentiments heard in Ecclesiastes are echoed in the book of Job. Further, in one telling sentence Paul directly links the meaninglessness of the world and the resurrection of Christ. This is important because what it tells us is that this sense of life's emptiness, the Void that is at its center, is not simply a postmodern experience; its deepest connection is not sociological but, in fact, *soteriological*. This gives us an entirely different way of thinking about this postmodern disposition.

Without the resurrection of Christ, Paul argued, his own work as an apostle would be futile, his struggles pointless, and not only would meaninglessness engulf him but it would blanket everyone, for if "the dead are not raised," he concludes, "Let us eat and drink, for tomorrow we die" (1 Cor. 15:32). His argument is rooted in the general order of resurrection, of which Christ's is the first fruit. It is the fact of this resurrection that makes the good life worth pursuing and that judges the alternative, which is a life of license, revelry, and emptiness. For Paul, it is this other order, entered finally through resurrection but that now penetrates this life, which gives it its purpose. It is this that explained why he was willing to have his life put "in danger every hour" (1 Cor. 15:30). It explains what energized him (1 Cor. 15:10).

## God Whispers in the Night

That there is a twilight knowledge of God that pervades human consciousness is indisputable from a biblical angle, and it is developed in two directions that actually also intersect. And the point of intersection lies in the conscience. From one angle, the dependability, orderliness, and beauty of creation all bespeak a Creator who is in covenantal relation with the creation (Gen. 8:21–22; 9:16). In his evangelistic address in Lystra, Paul spoke of this creation, as a result, as being a "witness" to God in that "he did good by giving you rains from heaven and fruitful seasons, satisfying your hearts with food and gladness" (Acts 14:17; cf. Ps. 19:1–6).

The other angle from which this is seen is the fact that the human being remains a *moral* being even in the midst of great moral disorder and confusion and, not least, even as a perpetrator of moral disorder. Indeed, that is what is at the heart of the sense of human futility and confusion. By creation, we are made for a moral world that we cannot honor but from which we cannot disengage. Paul argues that this fact is illumined both externally from the creation and internally from our own moral fabric. From the creation, "in the things that have been made," are revealed God's "eternal power and divine nature" (Rom. 1:20). As a result, we know God (Rom. 1:21), Paul declares. Yet this knowledge, which clearly is not saving, is no match for the willful disobedience of fallen human nature. The result is that God's existence and character are not allowed to order human life. The consequence of this is that his "wrath" (Rom. 1:18) is disclosed against every failure in the religious ("ungodliness") and moral ("wickedness") spheres, every failure to acknowledge God for who he is and to live life in a way that reflects his moral character.

The additional consequence of this willful disregard of God is the fact that life becomes empty and meaningless. Paul's actual language is that "they became futile in their thinking, and their foolish hearts were darkened" (Rom. 1:21). Fallen human reason is much given to fallacious ideas and fraudulent judgments because God has given it up to a "debased mind" (Rom. 1:28). Indeed, it is not only fallen minds that are subject to the curse of emptiness, but the whole universe suffers under this affliction (Rom. 8:20–21).

In a fallen world, Fate, Chance, Material, and Emptiness then assume God's place in life.[26] They become the organizing forces in the creation. The outworking of this inner hollowness nevertheless appears to be the essence of wisdom (1 Cor. 3:20)! However, the "more the unbroken man marches along this road secure of himself," wrote Barth, "the more surely does he make a fool of himself, the more certainly do that morality and that manner of life which are built up upon forgetting the abyss, upon a forgetting of men's true home, turn out to be a lie."[27] The vanity, emptiness, and futility of fallen reason are the affliction visited upon sinners by God's judgment. In every age, this has followed different directions. In the postmodern world today, whose center lies in the autonomous self, all of which is yielding a bountiful harvest of intellectual emptiness and moral disorder, this is not good news. What the postmodern world celebrates in its rejection of all absolutes and in its assumed right to define all reality privately is a sign of God's wrath (cf. Rom. 1:22).

People may plead ignorance in this situation, but Paul says they are "without excuse" (Rom. 1:20). Later, he develops this in terms of internal consciousness. Even the Gentiles who are without the written moral law still show that what it requires "is written on their hearts" because their conscience is actively at work within them (Rom. 2:14–15; cf. 1 Cor. 9:21).[28] It is no small scandal what Paul has to say here. What is revealed to all people everywhere? It is not that God is loving, though he is. It is not that he is accepting, though sinners may find acceptance with him. It is not that we can find him on our own terms, though he should be sought (Acts 17:27). No, what is revealed is the fact that he is *wrathful*. It is true that this disclosure comes alongside the fact that the creation also bespeaks his glory and the greatness of his power. Yet the greatness of his power and his glory do not obscure the fact that God is alienated from human beings. Indeed, his glory is precisely the reason that he is alienated! There is, as a result, already a faint foretaste of final judgment as the consequences of sin visit their retribution upon

---

[26]Karl Barth, *The Epistle to the Romans*, trans. Edwyn C. Hoskyns (New York: Oxford University Press, 1968), 43.

[27]Ibid., 49.

[28]James Q. Wilson has gathered considerable empirical evidence that points to the reality of this natural revelation. See his *The Moral Sense* (New York: Free Press, 1993).

the sinner. This is scandalous to a postmodern ear, but locked in that scandal is the key to meaning in the world, and in that meaning there is hope.

## God Reaches Down

### The Presence of Eternity

Given the collapse of Enlightenment rationality after the 1960s, what alternatives do we have for engaging what is ultimate, and how can we find the grounding for beliefs about truth and error, right and wrong? Or are we, like the postmodern nihilists and the earlier existentialists, obliged to live with the fact that there is no such grounding, that there is no objective truth "out there"? If natural reason cannot gain entrance to this world of what is ultimate—and postmodernists now see this to be a doomed and arrogant undertaking—then there remain only two other alternatives: the self and revelation.

Today, throughout America, as we have seen, the option that is being exercised is for the self, for Eros spirituality, for an assumed access that is unmediated into the sacred. In this new spiritual quest, it is the self that is the conduit into the spiritual world. It is through the self that seekers imagine themselves to be peering into, and experiencing, the eternal and by doing so hoping to find some meaning. And though its language was a little different, this was really the way the earlier liberal Protestantism traveled until it sank beneath the human debris of war in Europe and the Depression of the 1930s in America, incapable of addressing evil and suffering. It had no place to stand outside the culture. It could offer no judgment on human depravity. It had to assume the innocence of its own means of access into the divine, and that assumption simply blew apart.

The alternative connection to what is ultimate is, of course, revelation. In this view, it is not the human being reaching up to seize the meaning of life, or gazing into itself for that meaning, but God reaching down to explain life's meaning. In this understanding, there can be no speaking of God, no speaking of meaning, before his speaking to us is heard. This way was treated rudely by the Enlightenment luminaries because it both limited human freedom in shaping the meaning of reality and resorted to what was miraculous in the way revelation has been given. And it has not been treated any more kindly by the postmoderns for whom its grand, overarching Story is anathema and who do not believe that they can escape their own subjectivity. But this is the Christian confession.

The upward reach of Eros is always and forever blocked by the God who makes himself inaccessible to it. Biblical faith is about Agape, about God reaching down to disclose himself to those who could not otherwise know him, and about grace reaching those who otherwise could not be restored to him. This downward movement of Agape, this majestic condescension of God as he graciously makes himself known to us and in that knowledge gives to us an understanding of life's meaning, and therefore hope, is developed in the New Testament in terms of an *eschatological* redemption.

Thus, Christian hope has to do, biblically speaking, with the knowledge that "the age to come" is already penetrating "this age," that the sin, death, and meaninglessness of the one is being transformed by the righteousness, life, and meaning of the other. More than that, hope is hope because it knows it has become part of a realm, a kingdom, that endures, where evil is doomed and will be banished. And if this realm did not exist, Christians would be "of all people most to be pitied" (1 Cor. 15:19), because their hope would be groundless and they would have lived out an illusion (cf. Ps. 73:4–14).

For a long time in traditional systematic theologies, eschatology occupied the final section of the work and was concerned with "the last things" or "the end times," with matters like the return of Christ, the millennium, judgment, and the destruction of evil.[29] However, one of the great gains in biblical study in the last century was the realization that eschatology is not some final adjunct to the body of theological knowledge but more like a thread that is woven throughout its many themes. And it was the coming of Christ that radically transformed it. The conquest of sin, death, and the devil and the establishment of the rule of God do not await some future, cataclysmic realization. It has, in fact, already been inaugurated, although its presence is quite unobtrusive. As Oscar Cullmann notes, "that event on the cross, together with

---

[29]Pannenberg has correctly observed that because "God and his lordship form the central content of eschatological salvation, eschatology is not just the subject of a single chapter in dogmatics; it determines the perspective of Christian doctrine as a whole. With the eschatological future God's eternity comes into time and it is thus creatively present to all the temporal things that precede this future." Wolfhart Pannenberg, *Systematic Theology*, trans. Geoffrey W. Bromiley (Grand Rapids, MI: Eerdmans, 1997), 3:531.

the resurrection which followed, was the already concluded decisive battle."[30] Thus it is that, in the period between Christ's two comings, "this age" and "the age to come" coexist. As a result, eschatology, or the penetration of God's future into the current time of sin and death, is light that floods across a number of New Testament doctrines. Certainly in soteriology, everywhere there is the "already/not yet" tension that the presence of eternity in time creates[31]—or, more accurately, that the presence of Christ's victory that is already present amidst fallen human life creates.

In Paul, the present age is the age characterized by sinful rebellion against God, and the age to come is that in which Christ reigns. However, this reign has already begun redemptively in the regenerate church of which Christ is the head. The linguistic contrast between these ages is most explicit in Paul's prayer that Christ might be seen in his exaltation "far above all rule and authority and power and dominion, and above every name that is named, not only in this age but also in that which is to come" (Eph. 1:21). But, as Geerhardus Vos suggests, it is implied in a number of other passages: Romans 12:2; 1 Corinthians 1:20, 2:6, 8, 3:18; 2 Corinthians 4:4; Galatians 1:4; Ephesians 2:2; 1 Timothy 6:17; Titus 2:12.[32] This present age belongs to Satan, "the god of this world" (2 Cor. 4:4), but for the believer, this age or world has passed, its so-called wisdom has been exposed by Christ (1 Cor. 1:20). Paul is not always precise as to where the line lies between these ages. He can speak of the age to come as being in the future (Eph. 1:21; cf. 2:7) but he can also speak of it as being present (1 Cor. 10:11; 1 Tim. 4:1). It seems clear that for him it is not so much the language that matters but the *fact* that an inbreaking of divine power and grace has happened through Christ that is sending its clarifying, revealing light into life (Rom. 16:25; Gal. 1:12; Eph. 3:3), as it brings eternity into time.

Paul's Christology, therefore, also encompasses the language of the kingdom of God in the Gospels. To believe on Christ is to enter the kingdom and is to become a part of the age to come. Paul, however, expands this thought far beyond the personal and ecclesiastical. If

---

[30]Oscar Cullmann, *Christ and Time: The Primitive Christian Conception of Time and History*, trans. Floyd V. Filson (Philadelphia: Westminster Press, 1950), 84.
[31]This language is borrowed from Rudolph Bultmann, *The Presence of Eternity: History and Eschatology* (New York: Harper and Brothers, 1957).
[32]Geerhardus Vos, *Pauline Eschatology* (Grand Rapids, MI: Baker, 1979), 12.

Christ is the Lord whom every believer serves, the Head to whom the whole churchly body is responsive, he is also the Creator from whom everything derives its existence, the center without which there is no reality. Whether above in the starlit firmament or below within human consciousness, Jesus has "supremacy" (Col. 1:15–20).

In this fallen world, and in their fallen lives, those who are alienated from God are a part of this age, which is now passing. It has no future and there are intimations of that in the depths of human consciousness where a tangle of contradictions lie, for we are made  for meaning but find only emptiness, made as moral beings but are estranged from what is holy, made to understand but are thwarted in so many of our quests to know. These are the sure signs of a reality out of joint with itself. This is what, in fact, points to something else. These contradictions are unresolved in the absence of that age to come which is rooted in the triune God of whom Scripture speaks. He it is who not only sustains all of life, directing it all to its appointed end, but who also is the measure of what is enduringly true and right, and the fountain of all meaning, purpose, and hope.

CHAPTER 2

# Truth and the Supremacy of Christ in a Postmodern World

VODDIE BAUCHAM JR.

There should be little doubt that contemporary culture is in crisis, hurtling toward destruction. Questions that were once considered settled issues are now up for grabs. One hundred years ago, it would have been difficult to anticipate a genuine debate about the nature and definition of marriage, the morality of killing a child in the process of delivery, or whether a man is "too religious" for public office. However, these issues are not only being debated, but they are being practiced. Gay marriage is happening, partial-birth abortion is a common procedure, and political candidates regularly tone down their religious affiliations at the behest of their handlers.

It is in this context that the stark contrast between our culture and our Christ is seen most acutely. There has perhaps never been a better time to see and proclaim the supremacy of Christ, particularly in the area of truth. It is against the backdrop of this culture that calls evil "good" and good "evil"—where sin is celebrated and righteousness is mocked—that the Christ of Truth shines most brilliantly.

*Postmodernism* is an elusive term[1]—even for its advocates! But if we can say anything for certain about postmodernity, it is that the concept of accessible, knowable, objective *truth* is antithetical to

---

[1] See Douglas Groothuis, *Truth Decay: Defending Christianity against the Challenge of Postmodernism* (Downers Grove, IL: InterVarsity Press, 2000); Millard J. Erickson, *Truth or Consequences: The Promise and Perils of Postmodernism* (Downers Grove, IL: InterVarsity Press, 2001).

standard, postmodern epistemology. The ultimate goal of this chapter, however, is to give neither a detailed description of postmodernism nor an extensive defense of objective truth, but rather to celebrate and advocate the supremacy of Christ. Postmodernism is not supreme in this world. Christ is the one who is, and always will be, supreme. So if there is a conflict between Christ and postmodernity, Jesus wins all day, everyday, and twice on Sunday!

## Two Competing Worldviews

We can identify two major competing worldviews in our culture. Those two worldviews have been referred to by many different titles, but for our purposes I will refer to them as *Christian theism* on the one hand, and a postmodern version of *secular humanism* on the other. Recognizing that this is an oversimplification, it is still helpful to consider these as two broad, competing views on reality. My plan in this chapter is to address "life's ultimate questions" from the perspective of each of these two worldviews. We'll look at them through five major worldview categories, asking how they answer:

- the question of God,
- the question of man,
- the question of truth,
- the question of knowledge, and
- the question of ethics.

We will then turn to examine how these two competing worldviews answer the existential questions that each of us has.

### The Question of God

Christian theism answers the question of God by positing a necessary, intelligent, all-powerful being. Postmodern secular humanism, on the other hand, is fundamentally and functionally atheistic. Man is the starting point in this convoluted worldview. That is rather ironic, because while secular humanism is the overriding worldview of most of the people in our culture, the overwhelming majority of Americans report to pollsters that they believe in God.

## The Question of Man

Christian theism answers the question of the nature of man by seeing man as a special creation made in the very image of God (cf. Gen. 1:26–28; 9:6). In contrast, postmodern secular humanism sees man as a single-celled organism run amuck—a glorified ape who has lost most of his hair and gained opposable thumbs, a cosmic accident with no real rhyme or reason.

## The Questions of Truth and Knowledge

Christian theism views truth as absolute. If something is "true," that is, if it corresponds to God's perspective, then it is true for all people in all places at all times. However, postmodern secular humanism views truth differently. The previous generation of humanism—what we may call classic secular humanism—viewed truth through the epistemological lens of naturalistic materialism. It was inherently atheistic, as nothing could be known apart from this closed system called "nature." If nature is a closed system, then by definition there is no such thing as the supernatural. Such thinking is the functional atheism to which I referred above. The majority of Americans claim to believe in God, while espousing an epistemology that rejects the possibility of such a being. If nature is a closed system, then the God in whom one believes cannot possibly be the God of the Bible.

Despite the fact that postmoderns reject naturalistic materialism in favor of philosophical pluralism and experientialism, the end result is the same. Both worldviews reject the absolute, objective truth of God's Word and, in the case of postmodernism, objective truth in general. Classic secular humanism rejects truth in favor of matter; the postmodern version rejects truth in favor of experience.

Now if you believe in this sort of naturalistic materialism, how can you presume to refer to yourself as a Christian or anything like a Christian? Why say that you have a belief in God when, from an epistemological perspective, you have excluded even the possibility of God? Episcopal bishop John Shelby Spong, in his book *A New Christianity for a New World*, does just that, openly arguing from the perspective of naturalistic materialism.[2] He argues that what we need to do is move

---

[2]John Shelby Spong, *A New Christianity for a New World: Why Traditional Faith Is Dying and How a New Faith Is Being Born* (San Franciso: HarperSanFrancisco, 2002).

toward a non-theistic view of God. Spong claims that humans have evolved into the current theistic perspective, and we need to continue to evolve towards a nontheistic view of God. Here is a man who spent thirty years in pastoral ministry and was a lecturer at Harvard Divinity School, saying things such as:

> I do not believe that Jesus entered this world by the miracle of a virgin birth or that virgin births occur anywhere except in mythology. I do not believe that a literal star guided literal wise men to bring Jesus gifts or that literal angels sang to hillside shepherds to announce his birth. I do not believe that Jesus was born in Bethlehem or that he fled into Egypt to escape the wrath of King Herod. I regard these as legends that later became historicized as the tradition grew and developed and as people sought to understand the meaning and the power of the Christ-life.[3]

That's what happens when you cloak yourself in priestly robes but hold on to this kind of secular human epistemology that views nature as a closed system and man as nothing more than an evolved beast.

## The Question of Ethics

Christian theism views ethics—the question of moral rights and wrongs—as absolute, since morality is rooted in the eternal and unchanging character of God. Secular humanism and its postmodern ally, on the other hand, view ethics as completely cultural and negotiable. They claim that what is ethically right in one culture is not necessarily permitted in another culture, and therefore each culture negotiates its own ethical norms. As a result, there are many history professors who are unwilling to say that what Nazi Germany did in its attempt to exterminate the Jews was unethical, because secular humanism allows that somehow it fit within the framework and context of German culture and the negotiated ethics it had developed at that time.

## Life's Ultimate Questions

I now want us to look at how these two frameworks are worked out in real life. I also want to examine how we address the issue of truth, along with its relationship to the supremacy of Christ, in a postmod-

---

[3]Ibid., 4.

ern world. Every human being who has ever lived or will ever live has asked, is asking, or will ask four basic questions. They are the same questions no matter where you live (whether in Asia, Africa, Europe, or North America) or when you ask (whether in the first century, the twenty-first century, or, if the Lord should tarry, the thirty-first century). The four questions are these: (1) Who am I? (2) Why am I here? (3) What is wrong with the world? and (4) How can what is wrong be made right? While we may not all articulate them, it is in the soul of every person to wrestle with these four basic questions.

Allow me to answer these questions first from the perspective of our culture and then from the perspective of Christian theism, based on Colossians 1. If we ask our culture these four questions, here are the answers we get.

### Who Am I?

The answers provided by secular humanism to the first question are these: You are an accident. You are a mistake. You are a glorified ape. You are the result of random evolutionary processes. That's it. No rhyme. No reason. No purpose. You are ultimately nothing. This is the pathetic reality when evolution runs its ideological course. If the idea is carried to its logical conclusion, man has no more value than a field mouse; and if the field mouse is an endangered species that happens to share the man's property—guess who has to move?

### Why Am I Here?

Secular humanism's answer to the question, "Why am I here?" is that you are here to consume and enjoy. Get all you can. Can all you get. Sit on the can. That's why you're here. That's the only thing that matters. When the famous philanthropist John D. Rockefeller was asked, "How much money is enough?" he was as honest as any man has ever been. He responded, "Just a little bit more." Consume and enjoy. That's why you're here.

By the way, when you combine pleasure and consumption in a materialistic universe, you get terrible results. If I have no rhyme or reason for my existence—if I am no more than the result of random evolutionary processes, and I only exist to consume and enjoy—the only things that matter are whether I'm more powerful than you are and whether you have something I need for my enjoyment. If so, then it is incumbent upon me to take whatever I need from you in order to increase my own satisfaction.

Have we not seen this lived out in the world? Have we not seen the logical conclusion of this kind of social Darwinism? Have we not seen a culture that at one time said there is one race that is further evolved than all other races? They argued that because the Aryan race is superior to all other races, it is incumbent upon the Aryan race to dominate and/or exterminate other races in order to usher in the next level of our evolution.

Don't look down on them. Don't look down on their scientists and their biologists who viewed Jews as things and not people in order to justify their extermination, because that's exactly what our scientists and biologists do to the baby in the womb. The same concept of eugenics reduces the baby in the womb to an inconvenient lump of flesh. Even more sinister is the fact that severely deformed children are often exterminated in the womb due to their interference with our ability to consume and enjoy. At the other end of the spectrum of life, when people are old and feeble and the end is near, they not only have a *right* to die—now they have a *duty* to die. Just give them a cocktail and they can cease being a burden to their children, who are now taking care of them.

*Who am I?* According to the prevailing worldview in our postmodern culture, I'm nothing. *Why am I here?* I am here to make the most of it, to consume and enjoy while I can.

### What Is Wrong with the World?

If you ask proponents of postmodernism what is wrong with the world, the answer is very simple. People are either insufficiently educated or insufficiently governed. That's what's wrong with the world. People either don't know enough, or they are not being watched enough.

### How Can What Is Wrong Be Made Right?

The solution to our woes is more education and more government. That's the only answer our culture can propose: teach people more stuff and give them more information. How do we combat AIDS? We combat it through AIDS awareness. How do we combat racism? We combat it by offering anti-hate classes. What about the man who beats his wife? We send him to anger-management classes. Just give people more information and everything will be fine.

But if you take a sinful, murderous human being and educate that individual, he merely becomes more sophisticated in his ability to destroy. The world is far more educated today than it was during World War I. So how are we doing? Are we seeing fewer wars? No. Just more sophisticated killing techniques. Now we can kill more people in less time than ever before in history due to our "education."

If more education is not the answer, perhaps the solution is to be found in more governance. Really? There are two problems with that kind of thinking. First, *who's governing the governors?* In order for governance to be a real solution, there would have to be a special class of people who could govern the rest of us while having no need of governance themselves. The second problem is *the depravity of man.* Man will not simply improve as a result of being governed. On the contrary, he will just find loopholes and exploit them.

### Christian Theism and Life's Ultimate Questions:
### An Exposition of Colossians 1:12–21

The answers provided by postmodern secular humanism leave its adherents wanting and empty. How then do we respond? We open our Bibles to Colossians 1 to see how the Christian worldview responds to these same issues. Let's see how the supremacy of Christ can be applied to life's ultimate questions: (1) Who am I? (2) Why am I here? (3) What is wrong with the world? and (4) How can what is wrong be made right?

*Who Am I?*

Christian theism answers:

> [Christ] is the image of the invisible God, the firstborn of all creation. For by Him all things were created, in the heavens and on earth, visible and invisible, whether thrones or dominions or rulers or authorities—all things created through Him and for Him.[4] (Col. 1:15–16)

---

[4]Unless otherwise indicated, Scripture quotations in this chapter are taken from *The New American Standard Bible* (NASB).

Now some of you might be puzzled as to how this text is an answer to the question "Who am I?" The answer is that you cannot figure out who *you* are until you first discover who *he* is. Jesus is the image of the invisible God. He is the exact representation of the Father. He is the picture of God in human flesh. He is God on this earth. He is God with us, God among us. He is the Almighty, "for by Him all things were created." He is the Creator of all things.

Which things did Jesus create? He created all things in heaven and on earth. Thrones, dominions, rulers, authorities—all things were made *by* him. All things were made *through* him. This harkens back to John 1:1: "In the beginning was the Word, and the Word was with God, and the Word was God," which in turn harkens back to Genesis 1:1: "In the beginning God created the heavens and the earth." If we read on we find these marvelous words: "Let *Us* make man in *Our* image, according to *Our* likeness" (Gen. 1:26). So who am I? While our postmodern culture says that I am the result of random processes, Christian theism says I am the crowning glory of the creation of God (cf. Ps. 8:5). Christian theism says he knit me together in my mother's womb (Ps. 139:13). Christian theism says I am no accident. I am no result of random processes. Christian theism says that whether I am tall and beautiful or small and not so handsome, whether my body functions perfectly or is severely deformed, I am the crowning glory of the creation of God, and as a result I have inherent dignity, worth, and value. Christian theism cannot comprehend ideas like racism, classism, or eugenics.

Christian theism looks at the black man and the not-so-black man as equals. (You categorize the world how you want to; I categorize the world how I want to! But to my white reader, I want to say it's okay that you're not black like me; God loves you just the way you are!) Of course the question lingering when this issue is raised is *has that really been the case?* It's always hovering, even when people don't ask it. The question hangs in the air. I don't like lingering and hovering questions, so let's deal with this head-on.

Here's the question: *You say that in the context and confines of this Christian theism there is no room for this kind of racism, but we know for a fact that there have been cultures that on the one hand claimed this allegiance to Christian theism and on the other hand embraced racism and slavery. What are you going to do with that?* The answer is that I don't have to do anything with that. Narrative is not normative. Just because it happened doesn't mean it was right. Here's the point we need to reckon with: it stopped. What made it stop? What was the underlying worldview that rose up and said, "This is inconsistent"? What was the underlying worldview that said, "We are an exercise in cognitive dissonance"? What was the underlying worldview that rose up and said, "You cannot on the one hand claim allegiance to Christian theism and on the other hand despise men because of the color of their skin"? Was it Islam? No. Slavery is still rampant in the Muslim world. It was Christian theism that ended slavery in the Western world. Was it wrong? Yes, slavery in the Western world was wrong, but by what standard? Slavery was wrong by the standard of the supremacy of Christ and the Word of God.

Neither secular humanism nor postmodernism can grasp this truth—by what standard would either worldview have ended slavery? But when we grasp the supremacy of Christ, we cannot escape this truth. Who am I? Who are you? We are the crowning glory of the creation of God. I don't care what anyone has ever said to you. I don't care if your mother and your father looked you in your eye and told you that you were a mistake. You must never forget that you are created in the image of God as the crowning glory of his creation.

I will never forget the moment I grasped this for the first time. I spent much of my life wondering *why?* I was raised by a single, teenaged mother. She was seventeen years old when she became pregnant with me. She and my father were briefly married, but from the time I was about a year old, she was raising me alone in the drug-infested, gang-infested projects of South Central Los Angeles, where at that time the average life expectancy for a young black male was somewhere around twenty-four years of age. I have often asked *why?*—especially in light of our culture today that looks at young women in my mother's condition and tells them it would be irresponsible to carry their pregnancies through to term. But who am I? I am the crowning glory of the creation of God.

Regardless of the circumstances surrounding my birth or yours, regardless of the difficulties or infirmities with which you wrestle, regardless of your class or your station in life—because of the supremacy of Christ in truth, you are what the Creator of the universe says you are. And by breathing into you the very breath of life, he says you have value, dignity, and worth, and he says that I had better recognize that in you as well as in myself. And so we see the supremacy of Christ in truth, and we have the answer to question number one.

### Why Am I Here?

This culture basically says that there is no rhyme or reason, so we're here to make the most of it. Consume. Enjoy. That's why we're here. That is the overarching mentality in our culture, both inside and outside the church, resulting in unquenchable materialism and causing us to look at children as a blight and as a burden. While many in the poorest nations of the world talk about the number of children with which they can be blessed, we talk about the number of children we can afford. We have houses that are larger than they've ever had and families that are smaller than they've ever had. Our attitude toward children is "a boy for me and a girl for you, and praise the Lord we're finally through." Why? Because they get in the way of our consumption and our enjoyment. They cost too much. That's the fruit of postmodernism and secular humanism.

Christian theism looks at the question "Why are we here?" and answers it very differently. Again, we turn to the supremacy of Christ. Look at the next part of the Colossians text:

> All things were created through him and for him. And he is before all things, and in him all things hold together. And he is the head of the body, the church. He is the beginning, the firstborn from the dead, that in everything he might be preeminent. (Col. 1:16b–18 ESV)

"All things were created through him and for him." The ultimate purpose of all things is to bring Christ glory and honor, and that he might have the supremacy in all things. So who am I? The crown and glory of the creation of God. Why am I here? To bring glory and honor to the Lord Jesus Christ. That's why I exist. That is why you exist. That is why he breathed into us the very breath of life. He is to have supremacy and preeminence in all things. He is to have supremacy and preeminence in your life, supremacy and preeminence in the church, supremacy and preeminence over death and hell and the grave—

supremacy and preeminence over all. And because of this, the reason for my existence goes far beyond consumption and enjoyment.

I have the privilege of lecturing on college campuses all around the country, and this is an issue that I love to bring to the fore when dealing with college students. Most of them walk onto campus with one thing in mind: they ask themselves, "What can I get here that will facilitate my consumption and enjoyment?" That's why most people change their majors three or four times before they get out of college. Here's how they do it. They come to college with major number one—oftentimes a dream major. It has nothing to do with their aptitude. It's a dream. I meet students all the time. I shake their hand and ask them a couple of questions. I ask them where they're from, what they're studying, and how far along they are in their studies. And this is what happens:

I walk up and shake hands. "Hey, how you doing? Where are you from?"

"Oh, I'm from Podoke, Iowa."

"Great. What are you studying?"

"Pre-med and microbiology."

My next question is, "You're a freshman, right?" to which he or she responds, "Yes, how did you know that?"

I'm not talking about young men and women with the proper aptitude for such study. I'm talking about students who walk into college and choose a major simply based on the prestige of their prospective position. That's how they get to major number one, the dream major.

How do they get to major number two? They flip open *Fortune 500* magazine, find out who's making the most money with the least amount of education, and major in that. But then, after that too gets hard, they start to look around for yet another major.

And how do they get to major number three? Around the second semester of their junior year they walk into a counselor's office and say, "Excuse me. What do I have the most hours in? Yes, sounds like I'll be takin' that right there." By that time, the major of choice is get-out-ology!

But how about this radical idea: God knit you together in your mother's womb (Ps. 139:13). He gave you a unique mix of gifts, talents, abilities, and desires (Romans 12; 1 Corinthians 12). What would it look like if you grasped the supremacy of Christ in truth as it relates to your very purpose for existing, and saw to it that all of your education served to advance Christ's glory, supremacy, and cause here on earth? As Richard Baxter wrote:

> The most holy men are the most excellent students of God's works, and none but the holy can rightly study them or know them. His works are great, sought out of all them that have pleasure therein, but not for themselves, but for him that made them. Your study of physics and other sciences is not worth a rush, if it be not God that you seek after in them. To see and admire, to reverence and adore, to love and delight in God, as exhibited in his works—this is the true and only philosophy; the contrary is mere foolery, and is so called again and again by God himself. This is the sanctification of your studies, when they are devoted to God, and when He is the end, the object, and the life of them all.[5]

What if we saw our studies as stewardship? What if we raised our children not to go and do something just because it would make us proud but instead raised them so that they would discover the way that God has put them together? What if we decided to shepherd and nurture them in such a way that God could utilize the gifts he's given them for his glory? What if we continually taught them to focus on the supremacy of Christ in truth and how he relates to our very purpose for existing?

Christ "is before all things." Why did you choose your last job? Was it because of the supremacy of Christ in truth as it relates to your purpose for existing? Or was it because it paid you more than the job you had before? Pastor, how did you choose your current church? Was it because of a pursuit of the supremacy of Christ in truth in all things, even as it relates to your pastoral purpose? Or was it because this position is a little more prestigious than your last one? All things were made through him and for him. That means my life, my family, my ministry—everything that makes up who I am—must be characterized by a commitment to the preeminence of Christ.

### What Is Wrong with the World?

Obviously there is something wrong with the world. Let's look at the next part of the text for the answer in relation to Christ's supremacy.

---

[5]Richard Baxter, *The Reformed Pastor*, chap. 1.

> For in him all the fullness of God was pleased to dwell, and through
> him to reconcile to himself all things, whether on earth or in heaven,
> making peace by the blood of his cross. And you, who once were alien-
> ated and hostile in mind, doing evil deeds . . . (Col. 1:19–21 ESV)

What is wrong with the world? You are. "Hostile in mind, doing evil
deeds." Despite the fact that you are the crowning glory of the creation
of God, created to live and bring glory and honor to the Lord Jesus
Christ, you are instead hostile toward the One by whom and for whom
you were created. That is what's wrong with the world. In short, sin is
what's wrong with the world.

Many of the students who want to engage me in conversation are
first-semester philosophy students. (As an aside: there ought to be a
rule. You should not be able to talk about philosophy unless you've
had more than a semester of philosophy. If you haven't had any, that's
fine—you can talk all you want. But if you've had only a semester, you
are messed up. You'd be better off just not taking a philosophy course
at all!) These amateur philosopher-students love to catch me alone and
ask me standard questions such as, "I just wanted to ask you if you
believe in a God that is omnipotent and omnibenevolent, and if so, how
do you reconcile those beliefs with the issue of theodicy?" to which I
respond, "You just took a semester of philosophy, right?"

"Well, yes. How did you know?"

"Because if you hadn't, you'd have just said, 'If God's so powerful and so good, how come bad stuff happens?' But I'm not going to
answer the question until you ask it correctly."

"I worked on that all week! What do you mean, 'ask it correctly'?"

"You're not asking the question properly."

"What do you mean ask the question properly? It's my question.
You can't tell me how to ask my question."

To which I patiently respond, "I will answer your question when
you ask it properly."

When they are ready, I tell them how to ask that question properly:

> Look me in my eyes and ask me this: "How on earth can a holy and
> righteous God know what I did and thought and said yesterday and
> not kill me in my sleep last night?" Ask it that way, and we can talk.
> But until you ask it that way, you do not understand the issue. Until

you ask the question that way, you believe the problem is *out there* somewhere. Until you ask the question that way, you believe that there are some individuals who, in and of themselves, deserve something other than the wrath of Almighty God. When you ask me the question that way—when you say, "Why is it that we are here today? Why has he not consumed and devoured each and every one of us? Why? Why, O God, does your judgment and your wrath tarry?"—then you truly understand the issue.

The problem with the world is me. The problem is the fact that I do not acknowledge the supremacy of Christ in truth. The problem is that I start with myself as the measure of all things. I judge God based upon how well he carries out my agenda for the world, and I believe in the supremacy of me in truth. As a result, I want a God who is omnipotent but not sovereign. If I have a God who is omnipotent but not sovereign, I can wield his power. But if my God is both omnipotent and sovereign, I am at his mercy.

*Who am I?* I am the crowning glory of the creation of God, knit together in my mother's womb. *Why am I here?* I am here to bring glory and honor to the Lord Jesus Christ. *What is wrong with the world?* Me. I don't do what I was meant to do.

### How Can What Is Wrong Be Made Right?

How can what is wrong be made right? Look at the last part of the text, Colossians 1:22. The little word *yet* is one of the most beautiful words in the whole Bible. Can you imagine what life would be like if statements in the Scriptures such as we find in this passage weren't followed by *yet, nevertheless,* or *but*?

> Yet He has now reconciled you in His fleshly body through death, in order to present you before Him holy and blameless and beyond reproach—if indeed you continue in the faith firmly established and steadfast, and not moved away from the hope of the gospel that you have heard, which was proclaimed in all creation under heaven, and of which I, Paul, was made a minister. (Col. 1:22–23)

How can what is wrong be made right? We see two things in that last set of statements. First, we see that what is wrong can be made right by the penal, substitutionary, atoning death of Christ. And second, by that *if* statement (v. 23), we see that it cannot be made right by any other means—the supremacy of Christ in truth and redemption is found in his exclusivity. There is no other means by which man can be justified. "And there is salvation in no one else; for there is no other name under heaven that has been given among men by which we must be saved" (Acts 4:12). "For Christ also suffered once for sins, the righteous for the unrighteous, that he might bring us to God" (1 Pet. 3:18 ESV). "All we like sheep have gone astray; we have turned—every one—to his own way; and the LORD has laid on him the iniquity of us all" (Isa. 53:6 ESV).

How can what is wrong be made right? If you'll pardon the inevitable oversimplification, we can say that every other religion in the world basically boils down to this: "You need to have a religious experience, and from that moment on you need to do more good things than bad and then hope for the best when you die." They may differ in what that experience needs to be or how "good" should be defined, but ultimately, every other world religion is based on the necessity of doing more good than bad, without any certainty or security of an eternal destination.

I wrestled with that as a young freshman in college. I didn't grow up around Christians or around Christianity. My mother was a practicing Buddhist. I never heard the gospel until I got to college. Here's what I struggled with: I had been told that I'm supposed to have a religious experience, then do more good than bad, and hope for the best when I die. But I found at least three problems with this perspective.

My first problem: I can't be good. I tried. I can't do it. I'm incapable of it. I am totally, radically depraved, as the Reformers would say. Beyond a shadow of any doubt, I can't be good. Even when I do things that look to be good, I do them with wrong motives and destroy any good that was in them to begin with. I can't be good.

My second problem: What about all the things I did before my religious experience? Who, or what, is going to wash away the sins of my past? How long will I have to live in order for my good deeds—which we've already established as futile—to outweigh my bad?

My third problem concerned my assurance: How can I ultimately know that I've crossed the finish line? Is "hoping for the best when I die" the best I'm going to get? Am I doomed to wander through life hoping I make it in the end?

I found the answer to these three problems in the supremacy of Christ in truth as it relates to redemption. The Bible says, "For our sake he made him to be sin who knew no sin, so that in him we might become the righteousness of God" (2 Cor. 5:21 ESV). In days gone by God had been passing over, or overlooking, sins. And some were thinking that this called into question the justice of God: *God, how can you claim to be righteous and yet not crush Moses the murderer, or crush Abraham the liar, or crush David the adulterer? How, O God?* But in the merciful providence of God there came a day when God the Father crushed and killed his one and only Son in our stead in order to satisfy his wrath, "so that he might be just and the justifier of the one who has faith in Jesus" (Rom. 3:26 ESV). Was that enough for the sins of Adam, Abraham, and Moses? Can you hear the rhetorical questions from Calvary? *Was that enough for your sin? Was that enough for you to recognize the supremacy of Christ in truth as it relates to redemption?* There was nothing else that could have been done that would have allowed God to be both just and justifier. But in the humiliation and exaltation of Jesus Christ we find a resolution to the question, "How can what is wrong be made right?" Listen as the hymn writers proclaim:

> *What can wash away my sin?*
> *Nothing but the blood of Jesus;*
> *What can make me whole again?*
> *Nothing but the blood of Jesus.*
>
> *Oh! precious is the flow*
> *That makes me white as snow;*
> *No other fount I know,*
> *Nothing but the blood of Jesus.*[6]

And:

> *There is a fountain filled with blood drawn*
> *from Emmanuel's veins;*

---

[6]Robert Lowry, "Nothing but the Blood" (1876).

> *And sinners plunged beneath that flood*
> *lose all their guilty stains.*[7]

How can what is wrong be made right? The spotless, sinless Lamb of God was crushed, rejected, and killed to pay a debt that he did not owe on behalf of sinners who could never pay him back.

## Conclusion

If these two worldviews—postmodern secular humanism and Christian theism—are juxtaposed, something very interesting happens. With the former you are left empty and hopeless; man is left worthless, and you are left to pursue your own satisfaction and never find it. But with the latter, you are precious; you have purpose, and you are powerless—but it's okay because you were purchased. This is the supremacy of Christ in truth in a postmodern world.

Ultimately, this is what Christian theism tells us:

- Who am I? I am the crown and glory of the creation of God.
- Why am I here? I am here to bring glory and honor to the Lord Jesus Christ.
- What is wrong with the world? What is wrong is me, and everyone like me who refused to acknowledge the supremacy of Christ and instead chose to live in pursuit of the supremacy of self.
- How can what is wrong be made right? What is wrong can be made right through the penal, substitutionary, atoning death of the Son of God, and through repentance and faith on the part of sinners.

As we walk through the highways and byways and look into the lifeless eyes of individuals who have bought the lie, let us rest assured that by the grace of God we possess the answer and we are possessed by the Answer. The answer is Christ and his supremacy in truth. Let us weep that those who walk aimlessly through this life will never be satisfied with the answers that our culture has seen fit to give. The farther we have run away from the supremacy of Christ, the farther we have run away from the only thing that will ever satisfy and the only thing

---

[7]William Cowper, "There Is a Fountain Filled with Blood" (1772).

that will ever suffice. The supremacy of Christ in truth also means the sufficiency of Christ in truth. We preach Jesus and him crucified (1 Cor. 1:23). "For I am not ashamed of the gospel, for it is the power of God for salvation to everyone who believes, to the Jew first and also to the Greek" (Rom. 1:16).

This is the supremacy of Christ in truth in a postmodern, dying, rotting, decaying, and hurting world. Let us therefore embrace it and proclaim it passionately, confidently, and relentlessly, because, after all, that is why we are here.

Part 2

# Joy and Love

# CHAPTER 3

# Joy and the Supremacy of Christ in a Postmodern World

JOHN PIPER

John 17:13 is the seed from which this chapter grew up. Jesus prays, "But now I am coming to you, and these things I speak in the world, that they may have my joy fulfilled in themselves." The short form of this chapter can be put in two observations about this verse.

### The Short Version: Two Observations about John 17:13

First, even though this joy is Jesus' joy in doing the will of his Father, I think the source of the joy is something deeper. The ultimate source of Jesus' joy in doing his Father's will is seeing the Father's glory and being glorified with the Father. The perfect obedience of the Son is sustained by the joy that is set before him (Heb. 12:2), and that joy was his return to the Father (see John 17:5). So when Jesus says in verse 13 that he wants his joy to be fulfilled in us, he means that he wants the joy he has in his Father to be in us so that we would enjoy the Father the way he does.

Second, he says that the way he now conveys this joy to us is through understandable, Spirit-illumined, Spirited-ignited propositions. Verse 13: "*These things I speak* in the world, that they may have my joy fulfilled in themselves." These things I speak. And I speak in words and propositions so that my joy would be in you. "These things I speak." Things like, "I accomplished the work you gave me to do" (v. 4). Things like, "You gave me a people out of the world"

(v. 6). Things like, "All mine are yours and yours are mine" (v. 10). Things like, "I kept them in your name" (v. 12). Things like, "I am praying for them" (v. 9). Things like, "This is eternal life, that they know you" (v. 3). These things I speak—these words, these propositions, this understandable language I speak—that you may have my joy. I am not toying with you. I am not tantalizing you. These things I speak, and when the Holy Spirit comes he will take these things and reveal my glory through these things (John 16:14) and my joy will be fulfilled through these things in your hearts.

That's the condensed version of this chapter: (1) Jesus' greatest joy is in the glory of his Father, and (2) he shares this joy with us by means of understandable propositions (or Bible doctrine) about himself and his Father and his work, which the Holy Spirit illumines and ignites as the kindling of our passion for Christ.

The point is to simply affirm the precious truth of *doctrinally based joy* over against the postmodern debunking of propositional revelation and biblical doctrine and expositional preaching—as though there were some other way to attain Christ-exalting joy.

## The Long Version: Ten Steps

So what I would like to do in the rest of this chapter is give you the long version that basically builds an argument for the indispensable place of joy conveyed from Christ to us through objective, propositional, biblical truth illumined and ignited by the Holy Spirit. The argument has ten steps.

*Step 1*

*God—the Father, the Son, and the Holy Spirit, this one God—is the only being who has no beginning, and therefore everything else and everyone else is dependent on him for existence and for value and is, therefore, less valuable than God.*

Neither of these truths is part of the postmodern worldview— neither God's absolute, independent, eternal being, nor his supreme value above our own. But they are biblical and foundational. If we reject these or minimize these, the mission of Christ and the transfer of his joy to us will be undermined.

> Moses said to God, "If I come to the people of Israel and say to them,
> 'The God of your fathers has sent me to you,' and they ask me, 'What
> is his name?' what shall I say to them?" God said to Moses, "I AM WHO
> I AM." And he said, "Say this to the people of Israel, 'I AM has sent me
> to you.'" (Ex. 3:13–14)

In other words, God doesn't get his being or his character from anything or anyone outside himself. Because he never came into being, he
is not defined by anything outside himself. He simply is—and always
was and always will be what he is. "'I am the Alpha and the Omega,'
says the LORD God, 'who is and who was and who is to come, the
Almighty'" (Rev. 1:8).

And therefore, the difference in value between him and us is incalculably great.

> Behold, the nations are like a drop from a bucket, and are accounted
> as the dust on the scales; behold, he takes up the coastlands like fine
> dust. . . . All the nations are as nothing before him, they are accounted
> by him as less than nothing and emptiness. (Isa. 40:15, 17)

It is true that we have been made his children, heirs of God and fellow
heirs with Christ (Rom. 8:17). But we will never treasure *that* truth the
way we should until we tremble at *this* one.

Oh, that every person in this postmodern, self-exalting world would
come to feel and say, "I am totally dependent on God, and immeasurably less valuable than he. And this is the beginning of my *joy*."

### ENJOYING GOD'S SUPERIORITY

What words might the Holy Spirit use to open someone to the truth
that their inferiority to God is good news? Perhaps this: What if we
asked someone, "Would you want to watch a football game where
all the players were no better than you? Or watch a movie where the
actors could act no better than you and were no better looking than
you? Or go to a museum to see pictures by painters who could paint no
better than you?" Why are we willing to be exposed in all these places
as utterly inferior? How can we get so much joy out of watching people
magnify their superiority over us? The biblical answer is that *we were
made by God to get our deepest joys not from being superior ourselves*

*but from enjoying God's superiority*. All these other experiences are parables. God's superiority is absolute in every way, which means our joy in it may be greater than we could ever imagine.

### Step 2

*From eternity, God has been supremely joyful in the fellowship of the Trinity, so that he has no discontent or defect or deficiency that would prompt him to create the world.*

God does not act out of need. He acts out of fullness and ultimate self-determination. So Paul says in Acts 17:25, "He [is not] served by human hands, as though he needed anything, since he himself gives to all mankind life and breath and everything." And God says it like this in Psalm 50:12, 15: "If I were hungry, I would not tell you, for the world and its fullness are mine. . . . Call upon me in the day of trouble; I will deliver you, and you shall glorify me."

God says: You don't deliver me. You don't supply my need. I am not served that way. I give. I make alive. I sustain. I deliver. Whether I create or sustain, I act from fullness, not need. I did not create you because I have need. I am joyful in the fellowship of the Trinity. "This is my *beloved* Son, with whom I am *well pleased*" (Matt. 3:17). I love my Son. I am supremely delighted with my Son. And my Son has been with me from all eternity. And someday, if you trust him, he will say to you at the judgment, "Enter into the joy of your master" (Matt. 25:23). That is my Son's joy in me and my joy in him. And the Spirit of the Father and of the Son—the Holy Spirit—carries our joy completely from all eternity. We are a happy God. We did not create you out of need.

### Step 3

*God created human beings in his own image that he might be known and enjoyed by them and, in that way, display the supreme value of his glory—that is, the beauty of his manifold perfections.*

"Bring my sons from afar and my daughters from the end of the earth, everyone who is called by my name, whom I created for my glory" (Isa. 43:6–7). We were created not to improve God's glory but to reflect it back to him and put it on display. And he didn't give us minds and hearts to glorify him the way the stars and the mountains do (Isa. 44:23). They do it unconsciously as the work of his fingers: "The heavens declare the glory of God, and the sky above proclaims his handiwork" (Ps. 19:1).

But we were created with *minds* and *hearts*. Therefore, God commands us to *know* his glory with our minds and to *treasure* his glory in our hearts. "The earth will be filled with the *knowledge of the glory* of the LORD as the waters cover the sea" (Hab. 2:14). "Declare his glory among the nations, his marvelous works among all the peoples!" (Ps. 96:3). "I will manifest my *glory* in your midst. And they shall *know* that I am the LORD " (Ezek. 28:22). Paul says that God's purpose is to "to make *known* the riches of his glory for vessels of mercy" (Rom. 9:23). "God chose to make *known* how great among the Gentiles are the riches of the glory of this mystery" (Col. 1:27). "God, who said, 'Let light shine out of darkness,' has shone in our hearts to give the light of the *knowledge* of the glory of God in the face of Jesus Christ" (2 Cor. 4:6). We have been given minds to apprehend the glory of God.

And God has not just given us minds to *know* the glory of God, but hearts to *treasure* it and enjoy it. In the Old Testament, even the enemies of God knew how to use this to mock the faithful remnant. "Your brothers who hate you and cast you out for my name's sake have said, 'Let the LORD be glorified, that we may see your joy'" (Isa. 66:5). The glory of God is the supreme joy of his people—and even their enemies know it. That is why Jude said that God would keep his people for this great final experience—joy in the presence of his glory: "Now to him who is able to keep you from stumbling and to present you blameless before the presence of his glory with great joy" (Jude 24).

God created us to know and to enjoy his glory and, in this way, display its supreme value. We will come back to this in step five, but first there is a massive obstacle to our joy in God that must be removed.

### Step 4

*The Son of God, Jesus Christ, came into the world, lived a perfect life, died to bear the penalty for our sins, absorbed the wrath of God that hung over us, and rose from the dead triumphant over death and Satan and all evil, so that all who receive Jesus as the Savior, Lord, and Treasure of their lives would be forgiven for Christ's sake, counted righteous in Christ, and fitted to know and enjoy God forever.*

Oh, how I wish that at least here, at the center of the gospel, there would be common ground among those who claim to be followers of Jesus today. But that's not the case, and one of the reasons is that the postmodern mind, inside and outside of the church, has no place for the biblical truth of the wrath of God. And therefore it has no place for a wrath-bearing Savior who endures God's curse that we might go free. One of the most infamous and tragic paragraphs written by a church leader in the last several years heaps scorn on one of the most precious truths of the atonement: Christ's bearing our guilt and God's wrath.

> The fact is that the cross isn't a form of cosmic child abuse—a vengeful Father, punishing his Son for an offence he has not even committed. Understandably, both people inside and outside of the Church have found this twisted version of events morally dubious and a huge barrier to faith. Deeper than that, however, is that such a concept stands in total contradiction to the statement: 'God is love.' If the cross is a personal act of violence perpetrated by God towards humankind but borne by his Son, then it makes a mockery of Jesus' own teaching to love your enemies and to refuse to repay evil with evil.[1]

With one cynical stroke of the pen, the triumph of God's love over God's wrath in the death of his beloved Son is blasphemed, while other church leaders write glowing blurbs on the flaps of his book. But God is not mocked. His word stands firm and clear and merciful to those who will embrace it:

> We esteemed him stricken, smitten by God, and afflicted. But he was wounded for our transgressions; he was crushed for our iniquities; upon him was the chastisement that brought us peace, and with his stripes we are healed. All we like sheep have gone astray; we have turned every one to his own way; and the LORD has laid on him the iniquity of us all. . . . *It was the will of the LORD to crush him; he has put him to grief.* (Isa. 53:4–6, 10)

> Christ redeemed us from the curse of the law by becoming a curse for us—for it is written, "Cursed is everyone who is hanged on a tree." (Gal. 3:13)

---

[1]Steve Chalke and Alan Mann, *The Lost Message of Jesus* (Grand Rapids, MI: Zondervan, 2003), 182–83. For a persuasive and biblically grounded response to arguments against penal substitution, see Mike Ovey, Steve Jeffery, and Andrew Sach, *Pierced for Our Transgressions: Rediscovering the Glory of Penal Substitution* (Wheaton, IL: Crossway Books, 2007).

> For God has done what the law, weakened by the flesh, could not do.
> By sending his own Son in the likeness of sinful flesh and for sin, he
> condemned sin in the flesh. (Rom. 8:3)

Whose sin? My sin. Whose flesh? Jesus' flesh. Whose condemnation?
God's condemnation.

In our present fallen, rebellious condition, nothing—I say it again
carefully—*nothing* is more crucial for humanity than escaping the
omnipotent wrath of God. That is not the ultimate goal of the cross. It
is just infinitely necessary—and valuable beyond words.

The ultimate goal of the cross—the ultimate good of the gospel—is
the everlasting enjoyment of God. The glorious work of Christ in bearing our sins and removing God's wrath and providing our righteousness is aimed finally at this: "Christ also suffered once for sins, the
righteous for the unrighteous, *that he might bring us to God*" (1 Pet.
3:18). Jesus died for us so that we might say with the psalmist, "I will
go to the altar of God, to God my exceeding joy" (Ps. 43:4).

### Step 5

*The enjoyment of God above all else is the deepest way that God's
glory is reflected back to him. The enjoyment of God terminates on
God alone and is not performed as a means to anything else. It is the
deepest reverberation in the heart of man of the value of God's glory.*

We can do good works as a means to many things. We can speak
good words as a means to many things. We can think good thoughts
as means to many things. But we cannot enjoy God as a means to anything. We don't choose joy in God as an act for the sake of something
beyond joy in God. That's not the way joy works. You don't enjoy your
wife *so that* she will make your supper. You don't enjoy playing ball
with your son *so that* he will wash the car. You don't enjoy a sunset
*so that* you can become a poet. There are no *so thats* in the experience
of joy.

It's the very nature of joy to be a spontaneous response to something that you value. Joy comes to you. It rises spontaneously as witness to what you treasure. And therefore it reveals more authentically
than anything else what your treasure is. "For where your treasure is,

there your heart will be also" (Matt. 6:21). Joy is unique in its capacity to witness to what we treasure.

### There Is No Hypocritical Joy

There is no such thing as hypocritical joy. There are hypocritical smiles, and hypocritical laughter, and hypocritical testimonies about our joy, and hypocritical good deeds and kind words. But there is no hypocritical joy. Joy is either there as a testimony to what you treasure, or it isn't there.

God knew what he was doing when he created us to know and enjoy him. His aim is that we reflect and display the worth of his glory. God created us to enjoy him because joy is the clearest witness to the worth of what we enjoy. It's the deepest reverberation in the heart of man of the value of God's glory.

*Step 6*

*Nevertheless, the enjoyment of God in Christ is the spring of all visible acts of self-denying, sacrificial love that display to others the worth of God in our lives. God can see the reflection of his worth hidden in our heart's enjoyment of his glory. But God aims at more than hidden reflections. He aims for his glory to be visible to others, not just to himself. Therefore, God has constituted us so that our enjoyment of him overflows in visible acts of love to others.*

One of the clearest biblical witnesses to this truth is 2 Corinthians 8:1–2, where Paul says, "We want you to know, brothers, about the grace of God that has been given among the churches of Macedonia, for in a severe test of affliction, their *abundance of joy* and their extreme poverty have *overflowed in a wealth of generosity* on their part." First, the grace of God is revealed. Then joy abounds in that grace. Then joy overflows in a wealth of generosity—in spite of the fact of their "affliction" and "poverty." This is the way God made us: Joy in God overflows in sacrificial, self-denying acts of love. (See Heb. 10:34; 11:24–26; 12:2; 13:13–14.)

And these acts of love, flowing from joy in God, Jesus said, bring glory to him: "Let your light shine before others, so that they may see your good works and give glory to your Father who is in heaven" (Matt. 5:16). And what is this peculiar light that shines through deeds of love and attracts praise to God's glory and not to ours? It's the promise of joy carrying us over all obstacles to love. That's what Jesus said in the preceding verses: "Blessed are you when others revile you and persecute you and utter all kinds of evil against you falsely on my account. Rejoice and be glad, for your reward is great in heaven" (Matt. 5:11–12). This joy is the light that displays the worth of God through the deeds of love that the joy sustains.

There is no doubt that the postmodern world—like every world—must *hear* the gospel proclaimed and must *see* the glory of God flowing in many streams of radical, sacrificial deeds of love. My point here is that the enjoyment of God is the headwaters of all those streams, and that's why they make the glory of God visible.

*Step 7*

*The only joy that reflects the worth of God and overflows in God-glorifying love is rooted in the true knowledge of God. The only God-glorifying joy that flows from the mystery of what we don't know about God rises from the projection into the unknown of what we do know. And to the degree that our knowledge is small or flawed, our projections will probably be distortions, and the joy based on them a poor echo of God's true excellence.*

This is a response to the postmodern minimizing of propositional truth and biblical doctrine. The experience of Israel in Nehemiah 8:12 is a paradigm of how God-glorifying joy happens in the heart. Ezra had read the word of God to them, and the Levites had explained it. And then the text says, "And all the people went their way to eat and drink and to send portions [that is, to share!] and *to make great rejoicing*, because they had understood the words that were declared to them." Their great rejoicing was because they had understood certain words. Most of us have tasted this experience of the heart burning with joy when the Word of God was opened to us (Luke 24:32).

Twice Jesus said that he taught his disciples for the sake of their joy. John 15:11, "These things I have *spoken* to you, that my joy may be in you, and that your *joy* may be full." John 17:13, "These things I *speak* in the world, that they may have my *joy* fulfilled in themselves." And *what we mainly see in the Word is the Lord himself—offering himself*

*to be known and enjoyed.* "The LORD revealed *himself* to Samuel at
Shiloh *by the word* of the LORD" (1 Sam. 3:21).

### TRUE KNOWING GLORIFIES JESUS

The point is that if our joy is going to reflect the glory of God, then it
must flow from true knowledge of how God is glorious. If we are going
to enjoy God duly, we must know him truly. How can our joy reflect
the worth of God if it is not rooted in truth about God? If you say,
"My joy is in the journey toward knowing, not the arrival," you make
an idol out of the journey and you turn heaven into a disappointment.
Jesus is not honored most by the exploration of various christologies,
any more than your wife would be honored by your indecision concerning her character. Jesus is honored by our knowing and treasuring
him for who he really is.

He is a real person. A fact. A fixed, unchanging reality in the universe, independent of our feelings. Our feelings about him do not make
him what he is. Our feelings about him reflect the value of what we
think he has. And if our knowledge of him is wrong, to that degree our
enjoyment of him will be no honor to the real Jesus. Our joy displays
his glory when it's a reflex of seeing him for who he really is.

### THE ROLE OF MYSTERY IN OUR JOY

What then is the role of mystery in our joy? The Bible says, "Now we
see in a mirror dimly, but then face to face. Now I know in part; then
I shall know fully, even as I have been fully known" (1 Cor. 13:12).
If you get most of your joy from what you don't know about God,
God is not glorified in your joy. His Son and his Book and his world
are the revelation of his glory. He has made the knowledge of himself
possible. The function of mystery in the awakening of God-glorifying
joy is like the unexplored mountain ranges you can barely see from
the magnificent cliffs where you worship. You have seen much—if
only a fraction. You have climbed. You know these mountains. God
has made himself known in the mountain ranges of the Bible in such a
way that all the discoveries of eternity will be the revelation of the God
you already know truly in Jesus Christ. Therefore, the joy you have in
what you know of God is intensified by the expectation that there is so
much more to see. The mystery of what you don't know gets its God-

glorifying power from what you do know. God is not glorified by strong feelings of wonder that flow from ignorance of what he is like.

*Step 8*

*Therefore, the right knowledge of God and his ways is the servant of God-glorifying joy in God and God-glorifying love for people. Having ignorance of God and believing falsehoods about God hinder God-glorifying joy and God-glorifying love. And they hinder God-glorifying friendships and Christ-exalting camaraderie.*

I stress this because it is a very different take on the ground of friendship and camaraderie than you find at the Emergent Village:

> We believe in God, beauty, future, and hope—but you won't find a traditional statement of faith here. We don't have a problem with faith, but with statements. Whereas statements of faith and doctrine have a tendency to stifle friendships, we hope to further conversation and action around the things of God.[2]

I have two responses to this. One is to ask: Are there any statements which, if your friend really believes them, will destroy him? Statements perhaps like, "Jesus is not God." Or, "God is unjust." Or, "Jesus did not die for our sins." Or, "I don't need to trust Jesus to escape God's wrath." And if there are statements that, really believed, will destroy your friend, then denying those life-destroying statements and writing down the ones that lead to everlasting joy would sustain, not stifle, friendship.

TRUE FRIENDSHIP: SHARING A VISION OF GOD

The other response is to recall the distinction C. S. Lewis made between the love of romance and the love of friendship. "Lovers are always talking to one another about their love; Friends hardly ever about their Friendship. Lovers are normally face to face, absorbed in each other; Friends, side by side, absorbed in some common interest."[3] In other words, in romance, two sit across from each other and tell each other how much they like about each other. In friendship, they don't face

---

[2] http://www.emergentvillage.com/about-information/faqs.
[3] C. S. Lewis, *The Four Loves* (London: Collins Fontana, 1960), 58.

each other but stand shoulder to shoulder, facing a common challenge or a shared beauty or a great God.

For Lewis—and I think this is close to the biblical understanding of friendship—the greater the shared vision and the shared joy in that vision, the deeper the friendship. It's true; there is a risk that when you make a statement of faith about what you see in God, someone will turn away and say, "I don't see it," or, "I don't like it." At that point, courtesy and tolerance are possible, but not any deep friendship.

It seems to me that the "emergent" ethos uproots friendship from the solid ground of biblical doctrine and therefore preserves it in the short run as a cut flower. But in the long run, without the roots in shared biblical truth, it will not be able to weather the storms that are coming. And worse, while it lasts, it does not display the worth of God because it is not rooted in a true vision of his character and work.

The apostle Paul wrote in Galatians 1:8, "Even if we or an angel from heaven should preach to you a gospel contrary to the one we preached to you, let him be accursed." Friendship hangs on believing the same gospel. The main joy of God-glorifying friendship is joy in a common vision of God.

### Step 9

*Therefore, let us not marginalize or minimize healthy biblical doctrine about the nature of God and the work of God in Christ, but, rather, let us embrace it and cherish it and build our friendships and our churches on it.*

### Step 10

*And thus may the church become the pillar and buttress of the truth, and therefore of joy, and therefore of love, and therefore the display of the glory of God and the supremacy of Christ in all things—the very reason for which we were created.*

### A Personal Plea

I close with a personal plea. Probably most people reading this book are younger than I am, and many of you are young enough to be my sons or daughters. I am increasingly aware of that; the older I get, frankly, I like it. I am not upset about getting older. If what I have written here is true, I am fast approaching the face of Jesus and the voice saying, "Enter into the joy of your Master." This sense of age and nearness to the final river crossing colors how I think about the generation of my children (ages eleven to thirty-four). I don't feel like fighting with them. I feel like pleading: Don't waste your life on experiments. There are proven paths. They are marked out in the Word of God. They are understandable. They are precious. They are hard. And they are joyful. Search the Scriptures for these paths. When you find them, step on them with humble faith and courage. Set your face like flint toward the cross and the empty tomb—*your* cross and *your* empty tomb. Then, for the joy set before you, may a lifetime of sacrifices in the paths of love seem to you as a light and momentary affliction.

# CHAPTER 4

# Love and the Supremacy of Christ in a Postmodern World

D. A. CARSON

My generation was taught to sing:

*What the world needs now is love, sweet love—*
*It's the only thing that there's just too little of.*

Apart from the effrontery of telling God Almighty that in creation and providence he got his ratios wrong, the song does not acknowledge other things we need: holiness, joy in the Lord, obedient hearts. It does not even call us to recognize our creatureliness, which is our first responsibility. Even in the realm of love, the song never descends to the level of specifics. Contrast the sentimentality of the song with Jesus' robust insistence that the first commandment is to love God with heart and soul and mind and strength, while the second is to love our neighbors as ourselves (Mark 12:28–34). The song has just enough fuzzy sentiment that we can feel good about ourselves, but not enough truth to reflect much on what God says about love, or how he himself has supremely shown us what love looks like. In short, the song is neither ethically nor theologically serious.

By contrast, the five specific petitions found in John 17—petitions that Jesus, on the night he is betrayed, offers to his heavenly Father—though they are varied and interwoven, are all tied to some profound facet or other of the love of God. These prayers Jesus offers for his followers—and they are all bathed in the theme of love, not least the Trinitarian love of God. They are painted on a canvas of incalculable sweep.

Jesus' thought in these prayers is not linear. He circles around, adding perspective and layers of understanding as he cycles through his petitions. It is not long before we recognize that although there are five specific petitions, they are all woven together, such that none can be removed without unraveling all of them—and together they are anchored in the love of God and the supremacy of Jesus Christ.

I shall begin by identifying the *five petitions* that Jesus offers for his followers, the *ground* on which each petition is offered or the *reason* the petition is put forward, its *purpose*, and the manner in which it is tied to the *love theme* of this chapter. Only then shall I focus on the supremacy of Christ and its connection to the love of God.

## Jesus' Five Petitions

### Jesus Prays That His Father Will Keep His Followers Safe

First, Jesus prays that his Father will keep his followers safe. "I will remain in the world no longer," he says, "but they are still in the world, and I am coming to you. *Holy Father, protect them by the power of your name*—the name you gave me—so that they may be one as we are one. . . . My prayer is not that you take them out of the world but *that you protect them from the evil one*. They are not of the world, even as I am not of it" (17:11, 15–16).[1] The *reasons* why Jesus offers this prayer are that (a) he himself is going away, and so in his physical existence he will no longer be there to protect them (17:11); and (b) they, like him, do not belong to the world (17:16). Unlike him, of course, they once did belong to the world. But Christ had chosen them out of the world (15:19), and now, in principle, they belong to the world no more than he does, and so they will need protection from the world. The long-term *purpose* of this protection is (Jesus says to his Father) "that they may be one as we are one" (17:11). And such unity has as its aim, Jesus goes on to say, the display of the incredible truth that the Father loves them just as he loves the Son (17:23) and that the love of the triune

---

[1] Unless otherwise indicated, Scripture quotations are taken from *The Holy Bible: New International Version* (NIV).

God may be in them (17:26). So Jesus' first petition is that his Father will keep his followers safe.

*Jesus Prays That His Father Will Make His Disciples One*

Second, Jesus prays that his Father will make his disciples one. This oneness is the *purpose* of the *first* petition, the petition that God would protect Jesus' disciples; here it is the substance of the petition itself. That is what I mean by saying that these petitions are intertwined. Jesus prays,

> "My prayer is not for them [i.e., my immediate disciples] alone. I pray also for those who will believe in me through their message, *that all of them may be one, Father*, just as you are in me and I am in you. May they also be in us so that the world may believe that you have sent me. I have given them the glory that you gave me, that they may be one as we are one: I in them and you in me. May they be brought to complete unity to let the world know that you sent me and have loved them even as you have loved me." (17:20–23)

The first *reason* Jesus advances for this petition is also the *standard* he establishes: "that all of them may be one, Father, *just as you are in me and I am in you*" (17:21). The second *reason* Jesus advances is that he himself has already given them the glory that his Father had given him (17:22). We shall return to this intriguing thought in a few moments. The *purpose* of this petition, Jesus says, is "to let the world know that you sent me and have loved them even as you have loved me" (17:23), or, more simply, "so that the world may believe that you have sent me" (17:21). In the context of the Gospel of John, this not only invites the world to believe the gospel, making this a prayer with evangelistic purpose, but, even more fundamentally, it wants to see the vindication of Jesus. The world despises and hates Jesus so much it will be satisfied with nothing less than a cross. But if Jesus' prayer is answered, the world itself will learn that God sent him, that God truly loved Jesus' followers even as he loved his own precious Son. All this is the *purpose* of the prayer that the disciples may be one. And once again, we cannot fail to observe that this unity for which the Savior prays is inextricably entangled with the display of the incredible truth that the Father loves

Jesus' followers just as he loves the Son (17:23) and that the love of the triune God may be in them (17:26).

*Jesus Prays That God Will Sanctify His Followers*

Third, Jesus prays that God will sanctify his followers. "Sanctify them by the truth; your word is truth. As you sent me into the world, I have sent them into the world. For them I sanctify myself, that they too may be truly sanctified" (17:17–19). The *means* of this sanctification is "the truth," namely God's own word. In the context of the whole Bible, one cannot but remember the many passages in which God's word is his appointed means of making his people holy—whether a leader like Joshua (Josh. 1:8–9), an Israelite king (Deut. 17:18–20), or any faithful believer (Ps. 1:2). In the context of John's Gospel, the "word" primarily in view is the message of this book, the gospel itself. That is made clear by the way Jesus ends this petition: "For them I sanctify myself, that they too may be truly sanctified" (John 17:19). Jesus does not sanctify himself in the sense of making himself more holy. Rather, what he means is that he sets himself to do his Father's will, and his Father's will alone—and that means he readily goes to the cross, however repulsive and horrifying the prospect is. He does this for the sake of his disciples: "*For them* I sanctify myself," he declares. But the purpose of this is "that they too may be truly sanctified." None of us poor sinners can ever be sanctified, set apart for God, apart from what the Lord Jesus has done by sanctifying himself. By sanctifying himself, Jesus perfectly obeyed his Father and therefore went to the cross to bear our sins in his own body on the tree. That is the good news; that is the gospel. The truth of the gospel is what truly sanctifies us. The result, of course, is that we are no longer "of the world"—and that is why we will need protection from the world and from the evil one, which brings us back to the first petition. Moreover, such a marvelous conversion among Jesus' initial disciples, taking them out of the world and making them no longer of the world, is only the initial step to worldwide ministry that sees others converted: Jesus goes on to say, "I pray also for those who will believe in me *through their message*" (17:20). Thus, part of the *purpose* of the sanctification of Jesus' followers is their evangelistic faithfulness, which results in yet more conversions. For this Jesus prays.

### Jesus Prays That His Followers Will Experience the Full Measure of His Own Joy

Fourth, Jesus prays that his followers will experience the full measure of his own joy. "I am coming to you now," Jesus says to his Father, "but I say these things while I am still in the world, so that they may have the full measure of my joy within them" (17:13). In part, Jesus is saying something akin to what he said three chapters earlier: "I have told you now before it happens," he says to his disciples, "so that when it does happen you will believe" (14:29). Events were unraveling so fast before the eyes of the confused and still largely blind disciples that they had no category for a crucified Messiah. But by Jesus' saying these things now, by praying these things now, the disciples would soon learn, even if his words were opaque to them at the moment of utterance, that their Master really did know what he was doing, that his path to the cross was his Father's will and for their good, and all the joy that would be theirs would spring from what was still, to them, horribly confusing and disappointing. So here was the true *ground* of their joy: Jesus' own joy in doing his Father's will would be the very basis on which they would come to delight in salvation, in intimate knowledge of God, and share in the heartfelt pleasure of obeying the Father that is of the very essence of Jesus' own joy in his Father. This, too, is tied to the inner-love of the triune God. For although verse 24 does not use the word *joy*, it percolates through the lines of intimacy that the Son has always enjoyed with his Father: "Father, I want those you have given me to be with me where I am, and to see my glory, the glory you have given me *because you loved me before the creation of the world.*" And this is the joy Jesus now prays for his disciples.

### Jesus Prays That His Followers Will Be with Him Forever

Fifth, Jesus prays that his followers will be with him forever. It is worth repeating verse 24: "Father, I want those you have given me *to be with me where I am*, and to see my glory, the glory you have given me because you loved me before the creation of the world." The *ground* of this petition is the eternal love of the Father for the Son. Because the Father has loved the Son "before the creation of the world," he wants all those whom he has given to the Son to witness the Son's glory—and *that means that they must be where he is*. Thus the ultimate *purpose* of the petition is the glory of the Son, the final vindication of the Son, which is achieved because those the Father has given to him will see him as he is, for all eternity: "I want those you have given me to be with me where I am, *and to see my glory*." The Son had brought the Father glory on earth; the Father is resolved that all of Jesus' followers will witness the Son's glory forever. Small wonder that Jesus prayed, a little earlier in this chapter, "I have brought you glory on earth by completing the work you gave me to do. And now, Father, glorify me in your presence with the glory I had with you before the world began" (17:4–5). And this glory is itself the product of the *love* within the triune God from eternity past (17:24).

Transparently, then, even this slimmest of sketches of Jesus' petitions recorded in John 17 discloses their tight interconnections, and how each petition is in some way or other tied to Jesus' understanding of love, not least the love between the Father and the Son. At this juncture it will be helpful to trace out some of this Gospel's themes as they work their way into John 17, with the result that we can perceive some immensely enriching things about the supremacy of Jesus Christ and of love.

### The Themes of John's Gospel Woven into John 17

*The Supremacy of Jesus Christ in the Mediation of God's Love*

There are a lot of ways one could usefully get at this theme in John. But perhaps it will be simplest to pick up on a word that has repeatedly come up during the last few pages—the word *glory*. Within this prayer in John 17, Jesus uses *glory* or its cognate *glorify* as follows:

> "Father, the time has come. *Glorify* your Son, that your Son may *glorify* you [17:1]. . . . I have brought you *glory* on earth by completing the work you gave me to do. And now, Father, *glorify* me in your presence with the *glory* I had with you before the world began [17:4–5]. . . . All I have is yours, and all you have is mine. And *glory* has come to me through them [17:10]. . . . I have given them the *glory* that you gave me, that they may be one as we are one [17:22]. . . . Father, I want those you have given me to be with me where I am, and to see my *glory*, the *glory* you have given me because you loved me before the creation of the world" [17:24].

The important thing to recognize is that this glory theme did not fall from heaven into John 17. It is first introduced in John 1, in the Johannine Prologue itself (1:1–18). When we trace this glory theme, we quickly learn how it is tied to the love of God, to the cross itself.

The word *glory* first appears in John's Gospel in John 1:14: "The Word became flesh and made his dwelling among us. We have seen his *glory*, the *glory* of the One and Only, who came from the Father, full of grace and truth." John 1:14 is part of the block of verses, John 1:14–18—and these verses make several conspicuous allusions back to Exodus 32–34, those great chapters where Moses receives the Law, including the Ten Commandments, and shatters the tablets of stone when he learns that the people have sunk into debauched idolatry while he has been receiving the Law of God on Mount Sinai. I cannot take the time to trace all the connections between Exodus 32–34 and John 1:14–18, but it is important to identify at least three or four of them.

(1) John 1:14 reads, literally, "The Word became flesh and *tabernacled* among us"—and the giving of the law at Sinai includes the giving of the detailed instructions on how to construct the tabernacle, the forerunner of the temple. In other words, if the Old Testament tabernacle is supremely the meeting place between God and his old covenant people, and the place of sacrifice, so Jesus himself is the supreme meeting place between God and his new covenant people, and he himself is the sacrifice.

(2) In Exodus 33:20, God reminds Moses, "You cannot see my face, for no one may see me and live." Similarly, in John 1:18 the apostle writes, "No one has ever seen God." But John also adds, "But God the One and Only"—a clear reference to Jesus, the Word-made-flesh—"who is at the Father's side, has made him known." So although God in his unshielded splendor remains unseen until the last day, we have seen the Word-made-flesh, Jesus Christ—and he who has seen him has seen the Father (14:9). (3) In Exodus 34, when God permits Moses to look outside the cleft in the rock and glimpse something of the afterglow of the trailing edge of the glory of God, God intones several magnificent utterances to disclose himself, including the words, "The LORD, the LORD, the compassionate and gracious God, slow to anger, abounding in love and faithfulness . . . " (34:6). The pair of words "love and faithfulness" in Hebrew can equally be rendered "grace and

truth," and so rendered, they describe the Word made flesh, for he is "full of grace and truth" (John 1:14), and from this "fullness" we have all received, literally, "a grace instead of a grace" (1:16). The next verse provides the explanation, with its explanatory "For": "*For* the law was given through Moses [the very stuff of Exodus 32–34]; *grace and truth* came through Jesus Christ" (John 1:17). In other words, Jesus Christ, the Word-made-flesh, is the very expression of "The LORD, the LORD . . . abounding in love and faithfulness / in grace and truth."

With all of these connections between Exodus 32–34 and John 1:14–18, then, we cannot fail to observe one more. Moses, desperate to be anchored in God at a time of horrific rebellion among his own people, cries out in prayer, "Now show me your *glory*" (Ex. 33:18). God replies, "I will cause all my *goodness* to pass in front of you, and I will proclaim my name, the LORD, in your presence" (Ex. 33:19). Moses asks for glory; God promises him goodness. What Moses sees is something of the trailing edge of glory—but the words intoned emphasize God's goodness. So now in the Johannine Prologue, John writes, "We have seen his *glory*"—and anyone familiar with the Old Testament text will immediately wonder how, in John, God's glory is manifested in his goodness.

We do not have long to wait. After Jesus has completed the first of his "signs," the turning of the water into wine, John comments, "[Jesus] thus revealed his *glory*, and his disciples put their faith in him" (John 1:11). Of course, this was a miracle; there was something of glory in it. But it was a sign: it pointed beyond itself to the provision of the "new wine" of the new age that would be inaugurated by Jesus' death and resurrection. This glory theme keeps recurring in John, replete with evocative ambiguities, until John 12, when the ambiguities disappear. At the arrival of some Gentiles, Jesus knows his "hour," the hour of his death and resurrection, has arrived. Deeply afflicted, he testifies,

> "Now my heart is troubled, and what shall I say? 'Father, save me from this hour?' No, it was for this very reason I came to this hour. Father, *glorify* your name!" Then a voice came from heaven, "I have *glorified* it, and will *glorify* it again." . . . Jesus said, "This voice was for your benefit, not mine. Now is the time for judgment on this world; now the prince of this world will be driven out. But I, when I am lifted up from

the earth, will draw all men to myself." He said this *to show the kind of death he was going to die.* (12:27–33)

In other words, the place where God is supremely glorified is in the death, resurrection, and exaltation of his Son. Jesus' "glorification" is his return to the glory he had with the Father before the world began (17:5), but this "return" is via the wretched odium and ignominy of the cross. Here God's *goodness* is supremely displayed. God has indeed caused all his goodness to pass before us.

With this rich background in John's Gospel the glory theme takes on fresh dimensions in John 17, and these dimensions show how Jesus mediates God's love to us. Let me run through the relevant glory passages in John 17 one more time, but this time I will fill in further asides and comments:

"Father, the time has come {i.e., the time of Jesus' death and resurrection}. *Glorify* your Son {not least in this wretched cross, and in the vindication and exaltation to come, perfectly in line with John 12}, that your Son may *glorify* you [17:1] {for by this means all your goodness will be displayed}. . . . I have brought you *glory* on earth by completing the work you gave me to do {not only in the words and works of my entire ministry, including the "signs" that have pointed forward to the cross, but also now in the passion and resurrection that lie immediately ahead}. And now, Father, *glorify* me in your presence with the *glory* I had with you before the world began [17:4–5] {for the end of this "glorification" on the cross is the "glorification" of vindication, returning to the glory of heaven itself with all its unshielded radiance—the ultimate vindication of the Son}. . . . All I have is yours, and all you have is mine. And *glory* has come to me through them [17:10] {i.e., through the disciples, for the fruitfulness of Jesus' ministry is demonstrated in the disciples who follow him and are transformed by him, as they are taken out of the world and become truly his. They thereby bring glory to Christ Jesus.}. . . . I have given them the *glory* that you gave me {i.e., I have revealed you to them, in my person, words, works, and supremely in the cross and resurrection: here your glory, your goodness, are truly displayed}, that they may be one as we are one [17:22]. . . . Father, I want those you have given me to be with me where I am, and to see my *glory* {the glory of ultimate vindication}, the *glory* you have given me *because you loved me before the creation of the world.*" (17:24)

And there it is: all of this manifestation of glory, of the goodness of God, is displayed *because the Father loved Jesus before the creation of the world.* The thought is stunning. All this display of the glory of God focuses finally on the goodness of God in the cross and vindication of the Son for the sake of poor sinners—and all of it is grounded in the sheer love of the Father for the Son—the same love, Jesus insists, that the Father has for us (17:23). And thus Jesus himself becomes, uniquely, the mediation of God's love to us.

*The Role of Jesus Christ in the Trinitarian Experience of God's Love*

Here again it will be helpful to begin with an earlier passage in John's Gospel. This time I shall choose select parts of John 5:16–30, which is one of the most moving and insightful passages in all of holy writ on the meaning of Jesus' sonship. I cannot here take the time to expound the entire passage. I merely note that Jesus' words about his sonship are precipitated by a Sabbath conflict (5:1–18). Jesus claims that he has the right to act as he does because his heavenly Father "is always at his work to this very day" (5:17), and so Jesus, too, is working. But these words sound as if Jesus is claiming the very prerogatives of God, prerogatives that belong *only* to God. That prompts outrage on the part of his Jewish opponents: "For this reason the Jews tried all the harder to kill him; not only was he breaking the Sabbath, but he was even calling God his own Father, making himself equal with God" (5:18). They were simultaneously right and wrong: they rightly captured the drift of his extraordinary claim, his claim to have the prerogatives of God, but almost certainly they thought he was claiming, in effect, to be another god, a second god. Monotheism would give place to theism. They found the thought blasphemous, and so should we. There is but one God. Christians are adamant monotheists. But that means that in the following verses Jesus unpacks the unique nature of his sonship, the unique relationship he has with the Father. He is truly God; he has all the prerogatives of his Father; he is to be honored as God; yet he is distinguishable from his Father; and there is but one God.

We will follow at least part of Jesus' argument. *First,* Jesus claims to be utterly dependent on his Father: "I tell you the truth," he says, "the Son can do nothing by himself; he can do only what he sees his Father doing" (5:19). Some Christians, intent on preserving the full deity of Christ, are slightly embarrassed by texts like this. After all, they say, doesn't John's Gospel frequently stress Jesus' deity? After all, we are familiar with many important statements to that effect: "The Word was God" (1:1); "Before Abraham was born, I am" (8:58); "My Lord and my God!" (20:28). All true—and they are not to be weakened. Yet we also hear Jesus saying, "By myself I can do nothing; I judge only as I hear, and my judgment is just, for I seek not to please myself but him who sent me" (5:30); or again, "The one who sent me is with me; he has not left me alone, for I always do what pleases him" (8:30). The reciprocal claim is never made by the Father with respect to the Son. In other words, while the Gospel of John insists that Jesus is God, it insists, equally loudly, on Jesus' *functional* subordination to his Father.

But *second*, Jesus' dependence on his heavenly Father is utterly unique. After saying that the Son "can do only what he sees his Father doing," he immediately adds, "because whatever the Father does the Son also does." That is staggering. A baker's son may learn all that his father knows about baking; Stradivarius Junior may end up making violins that are just as good as those of Stradivarius Senior. But neither will be able to duplicate all that the heavenly Father does. I may be able to duplicate, in some small measure, certain things that God does. For instance, I may be a peacemaker, and since God is the supreme peacemaker, at a certain functional level that would make me his "son" (Matt. 5:9). But I could never say, "Whatever the Father does, I also do." The thought is preposterous. For a start, I haven't made a universe recently; I shall never be able to raise the dead on the last day. But Jesus says, "Whatever the Father does *the Son does also*." John has already established, for instance, that the preexistent Word was God's own agent in creation (John 1:1–3). This passage insists that the Son raises people on the last day, just as the Father does (5:21). So although Jesus is functionally dependent on his Father, his deeds and words, in John's Gospel, are finally coterminous with those of his heavenly Father. In short, Jesus does the kinds of things that only God can do.

*Third*, this Father-Son relationship is bathed in unfathomable love. John has already written, "The Father loves the Son and has placed everything in his hands" (3:35). Here Jesus testifies, "For the Father loves the Son and shows him all he does" (5:20). Indeed, springing from this love, the Father's will is "that all may honor the Son just as they honor the Father. He who does not honor the Son does not honor the Father, who sent him" (5:23). Moreover, the Son loves the Father no less than the Father loves the Son, even though the outworking of that love is slightly different. In John 14:31, Jesus insists that "the world must learn that I love the Father and that I do exactly what my Father has commanded me."

All of this is the understood precursor to John 17. It cannot now be surprising that Jesus in his prayer speaks of "the glory that you have given me because you loved me before the creation of the world" (17:24), or that he testifies, "I have brought you glory on earth by completing the work you gave me to do" (17:4). Here we witness the role of Jesus Christ within the Trinitarian experience of God's love—a love that is anchored in eternity.

### The Exclusiveness of Jesus Christ in Our Experience of God's Love

All that I have said so far constitutes the matrix of thought in John's Gospel that enables us to see the supremacy of Christ, the exclusiveness of Christ, in *our* experience of the love of God. To focus more sharply:

1) These truths enable us to understand *the perfection of the revelation of God in Christ*. If out of love the Father "shows" *all* that he does to the Son, and if out of love the Son perfectly obeys his Father and therefore does *all* that the Father does, then, springing from this inner-Trinitarian love, the words and deeds of Jesus are the words and deeds of God. Small wonder Jesus in John 17 prays, "I have given them the glory that you gave me, that they may be one as we are one" (17:22).

2) These truths enable us to understand that *the unity among his followers for which Jesus prays is modeled on the love-unity within the Godhead*. After the words just cited, "that they may be one as we are one," Jesus immediately goes on to say, "I in them and you in me. May they be brought to complete unity to let the world know that you sent me, and have loved them even as you have loved me" (17:23). In other words, when Jesus prays for the unity of his followers akin to the unity he has with his Father, he is not expecting them to somehow constitute another mystical Trinity. Rather, he wants them to love each

other with the perfection of love already displayed between the Father and the Son.

3) These truths enable us to understand that *the cross itself, the very foundation of all of redemption, is first and foremost the result of the love of the Father for the Son and the love of the Son for the Father.* The former guarantees that all will honor the Son; the latter guarantees that the Son perfectly obeys his heavenly Father. Jesus came to complete the work that his Father gave him to do (17:4). We so often think that the *ultimate* motivation behind the cross is God's love *for us.* I do not want to downplay the importance of that love; indeed, I shall return to it in a minute. But we must see that in John's Gospel the motivating power behind the entire plan of redemption was the Father's love *for his Son* and the Son's love *for his Father.* When Jesus found himself in an agony in Gethsemane, he did not finally resolve to go through with the plan of redemption by saying, "This is awful, but I love those sinners so much I'll go to the cross for them" (though in a sense he might have said that), but "Not my will but yours be done." In other words, the dominating motive that drove him onward to perfect obedience was his resolution, out of love for his Father, to be at one with the Father's will. Though we poor sinners are the unfathomably rich beneficiaries of God's plan of redemption, we are not at the center of everything. At the center was the love of the Father for the Son and the love of the Son for the Father.

When these truths have fully taken hold of our minds and imaginations, we are ready for the final truth:

4) These truths enable us to understand *something of the measure of God's love for us in Christ Jesus.* We have all learned to recite, "For God so loved the world that he gave his one and only Son" (3:16). So here: the world must learn, Jesus says to his Father, "that you sent me, and have loved them even as you have loved me" (17:23). The love of the Father for the Son is the love of one perfect Person for another; the love of the Son for the Father is the love of one perfect Person for another; and this in the mysterious unity of the Godhead. But in John's usage, this "world" that God loves is not understood to be a *big* place so much as a *bad* place. The "world" is all that is anarchic in the human domain, all that rebels against God. For God to love this world with the love that he has for his eternal Son is simply past finding out. The love

of the Son for the Father, though we understand so little of the Trinity, is comprehensible enough. But for Jesus to say to us, "Love one another. As I have loved you, so you must love one another. By this all men will know that you are my disciples, if you love one another" (13:34–35)— this is simultaneously incomprehensible and incalculably wonderful. We fall at his feet in adoration and worship; we are hushed, convicted, lifted up; we know ourselves to be immeasurably privileged, nothing other (to use Paul's expression) than the sons of God by adoption.

\* \* \* \* \*

Doubtless many who read these lines are aware that much contemporary scholarship on John's Gospel views this Gospel as irremediably sectarian. The dominant reason that is advanced is this: In Matthew's Gospel, Jesus' disciples are told to love their enemies (Matt. 5:44), while here in John they are told to love each other, and the enemies are not mentioned. Surely (it is argued) this reflects a community that has turned in on itself, a community that must therefore be labeled sectarian. But since our love for one another within the church is to be modeled on the intra-Trinitarian love of God, would anyone be so bold as to suggest that God's intra-Trinitarian love is sectarian? Contemporary sociological categories come nowhere near understanding what Jesus says in this Gospel.

Or consider what many ecumenical voices say about John 17. These voices tend to read a selection of lines from this chapter, and then say that if we do not sign on to the ecumenical movement, bury all differences of doctrine, and simply love each other for Jesus' sake, Jesus' prayer will never be answered. We have an obligation, they say, to ensure that Jesus' prayer is answered, "that they may be one." Otherwise Jesus' himself is frustrated by unanswered prayer. Such exhortations rarely wrestle with what this chapter says about God, about Christ, about Christ's mission, about the place this chapter has on the way to the cross, resurrection, and vindication of the Son, about the nature of the love between the Father and the Son. Moreover, Christians reading these words toward the end of the first century, when this Gospel started to circulate, were not wringing their hands and wondering how they could help poor old Jesus by encouraging the ecumenical movement along. They were exuberantly thanking

God that Jesus' prayer was being fulfilled before their eyes, as men and women were being converted from many tribes and tongues and peoples and languages, and were loving one another for Jesus' sake. Of course, this love is still far from perfect: nothing in these dimensions is perfect until the consummation. But Jesus' glorious prayer "that they may be one" is manifestly being answered to a superlative degree in the confessional church around the world today, as Christians bask in God's love and understand that all of our love is but a grace-driven response to the intra-Trinitarian love of God which has issued in the glorification of the Son by means of the cross, in the Son's perfect obedience to his Father, all the way to the cross.

Or what shall we make of postmodern voices that, in the name of love, deny the exclusive role that Jesus plays in mediating God's love to us? Will their siren tones increase love, or even our understanding of love? Sadly, no: they merely restore idolatry under a new guise. These voices are among the least tempered and least loving of our time, especially with those who do not agree with their vision.

Christian love is anchored in the Godhead, anchored in eternity, anchored in Christ, anchored in the cross. Other New Testament Christians, apart from the initial readers of the Gospel of John, understood these things, of course. "I live by faith in the Son of God," Paul writes—and then he cannot restrain himself, but adds, "who loved me, and gave himself for me" (Gal. 2:20). Again, we read, "We love, because he first loved us" (cf. 1 John 4:7–12).

*I love you because you first loved me: your love*
*With irresistible enticement paid*
*In blood, has won my heart; and, unafraid*
*Of all but self, I'm driven now to love.*
*I love because you first loved me: your love*
*Has transformed all my calculations, made*
*A farce of love based on exchange, displayed*
*Extravagant self-giving from above.*
*I love because you first loved me: without*
*Regenerating power provided by*
*Your Son's propitiating death, no doubt*
*My strongest love would be the mighty "I."*
    *Your self-originating love's alone—*
    *The motive, standard, power of my own.*

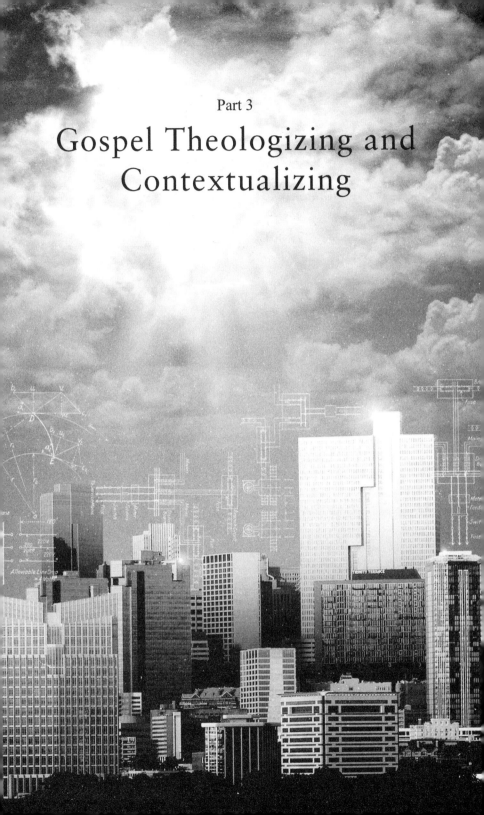

Part 3

# Gospel Theologizing and Contextualizing

# CHAPTER 5

# The Gospel and the Supremacy of Christ in a Postmodern World

TIM KELLER

## A Crisis for Evangelism

Our current cultural situation poses a crisis for the way evangelicals have been doing evangelism for the past 150 years—causing us to raise crucial questions like: How do we do evangelism today? How do we get the gospel across in a postmodern world?

In 1959 Martyn Lloyd-Jones gave a series of messages on revival. One of his expositions was on Mark 9, where Jesus comes off the mountain of transfiguration and discovers his disciples trying unsuccessfully to exorcise a demon from a boy. After he rids the youth of the demonic presence, the disciples ask him, "Why could we not cast it out?" Jesus answers, "This kind cannot be driven out by anything but prayer" (Mark 9:28–29). Jesus was teaching his disciples that their ordinary methods did not work for "*this kind.*" Lloyd-Jones went on to apply this to the church:

> Here, in this boy, I see the modern world, and in the disciples I see the Church of God. . . . I see a very great difference between today and two hundred years ago, or indeed even one hundred years ago. The difficulty in those earlier times was that men and women were in a state of apathy. They were more or less asleep. . . . [T]here was no general denial of Christian truth. It was just that people did not trouble to practise it. . . . [A]ll you had to do then was to awaken them and to rouse them. . . .

> But the question is whether that is still the position. . . . What is
> 'this kind'? . . . [T]he kind of problem facing us is altogether deeper
> and more desperate. . . . [T]he very belief in God has virtually gone. . . .
> [T]he average man today believes that all this belief about God and
> religion and salvation . . . [is] an incubus on human nature all through
> the centuries. . . .
>
> It is no longer merely a question of immorality. This has become
> an amoral or a non-moral society. The very category of morality is not
> recognised. . . .
>
> The power that the disciples had was a good power, and it was able
> to do good work in casting out the feeble devils, but it was no value in
> the case of that boy.[1]

Put simply, Jesus is saying, *the demon is in too deep for your ordinary way of doing ministry.* It is intriguing that Lloyd-Jones said this some time before Lesslie Newbigin began to propound the thesis that Western society was a mission field again.[2] Indeed it was perhaps the most challenging mission field yet, because no one had ever had to evangelize on a large scale a society that *used* to be Christian. Certainly there have been many times in the past when the church was in serious decline, and revival revitalized the faith and society. But in those times society was still nominally Christian. There hadn't been a wholesale erosion of the very concepts of God and truth and of the basic reliability and wisdom of the Bible. Things are different now.

Inoculation introduces a mild form of a disease into a body, thereby stimulating the growth of antibodies and rendering the person immune to getting a full-blown version of the sickness. In the same way, *post*-Christian society contains unique resistance and "antibodies" against full-blown Christianity. For example, the memory of sustained injustices that flourished under more Christianized Western societies has become an antibody against the gospel. *Christianity was big back when blacks had to sit on the back of the bus and when women were beaten up by men without consequences. We've tried out a Christian society and it wasn't so hot. Been there. Done that.* In a society like ours, most people only know of either a very mild, nominal Christianity or a separatist, legalistic Christianity. Neither of these is, may we say, "the real

---

[1]D. Martyn Lloyd-Jones, *Revival* (Wheaton, IL: Crossway Books, 1987), 9, 13–15.
[2]See Lesslie Newbigin, *Foolishness to the Greeks* (Grand Rapids, MI: Eerdmans, 1986) and *The Gospel in a Pluralistic Society* (Grand Rapids, MI: Eerdmans, 1989).

thing." But exposure to them creates spiritual antibodies, as it were, making the listener extremely resistant to the gospel. These antibodies are now everywhere in our society.

During the rest of his sermon on Mark 9, Lloyd-Jones concludes that the evangelism and church-growth methods of the past couple of centuries, while perfectly good for their time (he was careful to say that), would no longer work. What was needed now was something far more comprehensive and far-reaching than a new set of evangelistic programs.

I believe that Lloyd-Jones's diagnosis is completely on target. Richard Fletcher's *The Barbarian Conversion* traces the way in which Christians evangelized in a pagan context from A.D. 500–1500.[3] During that time major swaths of Europe (especially the countryside rather than the cities) remained pre-Christian pagan. They lacked the basic "worldview furniture" of the Christian mind. They did not have a Christian understanding of God, truth, or sin, or of peculiar Christian ethical practices. Evangelism and Christian instruction were a very long and comprehensive process.

But eventually nearly everyone in Europe (and then in North America) was born into a world that was (at least intellectually) Christian. People were educated into a basic Christian-thought framework—a Christian view of God, of soul and body, of heaven and hell, of rewards and punishments, of the Ten Commandments and the Sermon on the Mount. And that is why the church could make evangelism into both a simpler and a more subjective process than that practiced by previous generations. The people believed in sin, but they hadn't come to a profound conviction that *they* were helpless sinners. They believed in Jesus as the Son of God who died for sin, but they hadn't come to cling to him personally and wholly for their own salvation and life. They needed to come to a deep personal conviction of sin and to an experience of God's grace through Christ. They had a Christian mind and conscience, but they didn't have a Christian heart. The need, then, was for some kind of campaign or program that roused and shook people—taking what they already basically believed and making it vivid and personal for them, seeking an individual response of repentance and faith.

---

[3]Richard Fletcher, *The Barbarian Conversion: From Paganism to Christianity* (Berkeley: University of California Press, 1999).

Since the end of the "Barbarian Conversion," then, evangelism has shrunk into a program with most of the emphasis being on individual experience. The programs have ranged from preaching-and-music revival seasons, to one-on-one witnessing, to small-group processes. I agree with Lloyd-Jones that there was nothing wrong with these methods as far as they went and in their day. But now *this kind* won't be effectively addressed by that older approach.

### No More Magic Bullets

Some might respond that Lloyd-Jones has not been proven right. Isn't evangelical Christianity growing—at least in North America? Look at all the megachurches spouting up! But we must remember that the new situation Lloyd-Jones was describing has spread in stages. It was in Europe before North America. It was in cities before it was in the rest of the society. In the United States it has strengthened in the Northeast and the West Coast first. In many places, especially in the South and Midwest, there is still a residue of more conservative society where people maintain traditional values. Many of these people are therefore still reachable with the fairly superficial, older evangelism programs of the past. And if we are honest, we should admit that many churches are growing large without any evangelism at all. If a church can present unusually good preaching and family ministries and programming, it can easily attract the remaining traditional people and siphon off Christians from all the other churches in a thirty-mile radius. This is easier now than ever because people are very mobile, less tied into their local communities, and less loyal to institutions that don't meet their immediate needs. But despite the growth of megachurches through these dynamics, there is no evidence that the number of churchgoers in the United States is significantly increasing.[4]

What *is* clear is that the number of secular people professing "no religious preference" is growing rapidly. Michael Wolff, writing in *New York* Magazine, captures the growing divide:

> [There is a] fundamental schism in American cultural, political, and economic life. There's the quicker-growing, economically vibrant . . . morally relativist, urban-oriented, culturally adventuresome, sexu-

---

[4]See, for example, http://ww.theamericanchurch.org/facts/1.htm.

ally polymorphous, and ethnically diverse nation. . . . And there's the small-town, nuclear-family, religiously oriented, white-centric other America . . . [with] its diminishing cultural and economic force. . . . [T]wo countries. . . .[5]

So Lloyd-Jones is right that *the demon is in too deep for your ordinary way of doing ministry*—especially in more secular, pluralistic Europe and in the parts of the United States that are similar. In the Christ-haunted places of the West you can still get a crowd without evangelism or with the older approaches. But the traditional pockets of Western society simply are not growing.

I will put my neck on the line and go so far as to say that in my almost thirty-five years in full-time ministry I've seen nearly all the older evangelism programs fade away as they have proved less and less effective. Dwight Moody pioneered the mass preaching crusade in the late nineteenth century, and Billy Graham brought it to its state of greatest efficiency and success, but few are looking in that direction for reaching our society with the gospel.

In the latter part of the twentieth century there were a number of highly effective, short, memorizable, bullet-pointed gospel presentations written for individual lay Christians to use in personal evangelism. Programs were developed for training lay people to use the presentations door-to-door, or in "contact" evangelism in public places, or with visitors to church, or in personal relationships. These have all been extremely helpful, but the churches I know that have used the same program in the same place for decades have seen steadily diminishing fruit.

The next wave of evangelism programming was the "seeker service" model developed by many churches, especially large ones. It is far too early to say that this methodology is finished, and yet younger ministers and church leaders are wont to say that it is too geared to people with a traditional, bourgeoisie, still-Christ-haunted mindset to operate. In many parts of society that kind of person is disappearing.

Today the main programmatic "hope" for churches seeking to be evangelistic is the "Alpha" method which comes out of Holy Trinity

---

[5]Michael Wolff, "The Party Line," *New York* Magazine (Feb. 26, 2001): 19. Online at http://nymag.com/nymetro/news/media/columns/medialife/4407/index1.html.

Anglican Church in London.[6] There are good reasons why this more communal, process-oriented approach has been so fruitful, but I believe that the same principle will hold true, even for Alpha. There is no "magic bullet." You can't simply graft a program (like Alpha or its counterparts) onto your existing church-as-usual. You can't just whip up a new gospel presentation, design a program, hire the staff, and try to get people in the door. *The whole church and everything it does is going to have to change.* The demon's in too deep for the older ways.

In fact, things are more difficult than they were in Lloyd-Jones's lifetime. He was facing what has been called a "modern" culture, and we face a "postmodern" one—making our evangelism methods even more obsolete. It is not my job to look at the "modern vs. postmodern" distinction in any detail, but I think most would agree that the postmodern mindset is associated with at least three problems. First, there's a *truth* problem. All claims of truth are seen not as that which corresponds to reality but primarily as constraints aimed to siphon power off toward the claimer. Second, there's the *guilt* problem. Though guilt was mainly seen as a neurosis in the modern era (with the reign of Freud), it was still considered a problem. Almost all the older gospel presentations assume an easily accessed sense of guilt and moral shortcoming in the listener. But today that is increasingly absent. Third, there is now a *meaning* problem. Today there's enormous skepticism that texts and words can accurately convey meaning. If we say, "Here is a biblical text and this is what it says," the response will be, "Who are you to say this is the right interpretation? Textual meanings are unstable."

So how do we get the gospel across in the postmodern world? *The gospel* and *the fact that we are now a church on a mission field* will dictate that almost everything the church does will have to be changed. But that is too broad a statement to be of any help, so I will lay out six ways in which the church will have to change. Each of these factors has parallels in the account of Jonah and his mission to the great pagan metropolis of Nineveh.[7]

---

[6]See www.alpha.org.
[7]I will ground the six factors in the Jonah text, but the following should not be seen as an effort to carefully or thoroughly expound the book of Jonah.

## Gospel Theologizing

Jonah 1:1–2: "The word of the Lord came to Jonah . . . saying, 'Go to . . . Nineveh and preach'" (NIV). For a long time I understood the "gospel" as being just elementary truths, the doctrinal minimum requirement for entering the faith. "Theology," I thought, was the advanced, meatier, deeper, biblical stuff. How wrong I was! *All* theology must be an exposition of the gospel, especially in the postmodern age.

A good example of this is found in Mark Thompson's book, *A Clear and Present Word*.[8] Thompson first describes our cultural context in which people believe all meanings are unstable and all texts are indeterminate. He then develops a Christian theology of language. This is certainly not elementary stuff. He begins by looking at the Trinity. Each person—Father, Son, and Holy Spirit—seeks not his own glory but only to give glory and honor to the others. Each one is pouring love and joy into the heart of the other. Why would a God like this create a universe? As Jonathan Edwards so famously reasoned, it couldn't be in order to get love and adoration, since as a triune God he already had that in himself.[9] Rather, he created a universe to spread the glory and joy he already had. He created other beings to communicate his own love and glory to them and have them communicate it back to him, so they (we!) could step into the great Dance, the circle of love and glory and joy that he already had.

Words and language, then, are ingredients in the self-giving of the divine persons to each other and therefore to us. In creation and redemption God gives us life and being through his Word. We can't live without words, and we can't be saved without *the* Word, Jesus Christ. Human language, then, isn't an insufficient human construct but an imperfectly utilized gift from God. Thompson concludes:

> The [gospel is that the] right and proper judgment of God against our rebellion has not been overturned; it has been exhausted, embraced in full by the eternal Son of God himself. . . .

---

[8] Mark D. Thompson, *A Clear and Present Word: The Clarity of Scripture*, New Studies in Biblical Theology, ed. D. A. Carson (Downers Grove, IL: InterVarsity Press, 2006).
[9] See the singular "The Dissertation Concerning the End for Which God Created the World," in *The Works of Jonathan Edwards*, vol. 8, *Ethical Writings*, ed. Paul Ramsey (New Haven, CT: Yale University Press, 1989).

God uses words in the service of his intention to rescue men and women, drawing them into fellowship with him and preparing a new creation as an appropriate venue for the enjoyment of that fellowship. In other words, the knowledge of God that is the goal of God's speaking ought never to be separated from the centerpiece of Christian theology; namely, the salvation of sinners.[10]

This is certainly not elementary theologizing, but a grounding of even the very philosophy and understanding of human language in the gospel. The Word of the Lord (as we see in Jonah 1:1) is never abstract theologizing, but is a life-changing message about the severity and mercy of God.

Why is this so important? First, in a time in which there is so much ignorance of the basic Christian worldview, we have to get to the core of things, the gospel, every time we speak. Second, the gospel of salvation doesn't really relate to theology like the first steps relate to the rest of the stairway but more like the hub relates through the spokes to the rest of the wheel. The gospel of a glorious, other-oriented triune God giving himself in love to his people in creation and redemption and re-creation *is* the core of every doctrine—of the Bible, of God, of humanity, of salvation, of ecclesiology, of eschatology. However, third, we must recognize that in a postmodern society where everyone is against abstract speculation, we will be ignored unless we ground all we say in the gospel. Why? The postmodern era has produced in its citizens a hunger for beauty and justice. This is not an abstract culture, but a culture of story and image. The gospel is not less than a set of revealed propositions (God, sin, Christ, faith), but it is *more*. It is also a narrative (creation, fall, redemption, restoration.) Unfortunately, there are people under the influence of postmodernism who are so obsessed with narrative *rather* than propositions that they are rejecting inerrancy, are moving toward open theism, and so on. But to some extent they are reacting to abstract theologizing that was not grounded in the gospel and real history. They want to put more emphasis on the actual history of salvation, on the coming of the kingdom, on the importance of community, and on the renewal of the material creation.

But we must not pit systematic theology and biblical theology against each other, nor the substitutionary atonement against the king-

---

[10]Thompson, *A Clear and Present Word*, 56, 65.

dom of God. Look again at the above quote from Mark Thompson and you will see a skillful blending of both individual salvation from God's wrath and the creation of a new community and material world. This world is reborn along with us—cleansed, beautified, perfected, and purified of all death, disease, brokenness, injustice, poverty, deformity. It is not just tacked on as a chapter in abstract "eschatology," but is the only appropriate venue for enjoyment of that fellowship with God brought to us by grace through our union with Christ.

In general, I don't think we've done a good job at developing ways of communicating the gospel that include both salvation from wrath by propitiation *and* the restoration of all things. Today, writing accessible presentations of the gospel should not be the work of marketers but the work of our best theologians.

## Gospel Realizing

When God called Jonah to go to Nineveh the first time, Jonah ran in the other direction. Why? The reader assumes it was just fear, but chapter 4 reveals that there was also a lot of hostility in Jonah toward the Assyrians and Ninevites. I believe the reason he did not have pity on them was that he did not sufficiently realize that *he* was nothing but a sinner saved by sheer grace. So he ran away from God—and you know the rest of the story. He was cast into the deep and saved by God from drowning by being swallowed by a great fish. In the second chapter we see Jonah praying, and his prayer ends with the phrase "Salvation is of the LORD !" (2:9). My teacher Ed Clowney used to say that this was the central verse of the Bible. It is an expression of the gospel. Salvation is *from* and *of* the Lord and no one else. Period.

But as a prophet, doesn't Jonah know this? He knows it—and yet he doesn't know it. For eighteen years I lived in apartment buildings with vending machines. Very often you put the coins in but nothing comes out. You have to shake or hit the machine on the side till the coins finally drop down and then out comes the soda. My wife, Kathy, believes this is a basic parable for all ministry. Martin Luther said that the purpose of ministry was not only to make the gospel clear, but to beat it into your people's heads (and your own!) continually.[11] You

---

[11] "This is the truth of the gospel. It is also the principal article of all Christian doctrine, whereby the knowledge of all goodness consisteth. Most necessary it is therefore, that we should know this article well, teach it to others and beat it into their heads continually."

might be able to get an *A* on your justification-by-faith test, but if there is not radical, concrete growth in humble love toward everyone (even your enemies), you don't *really* know you are a *sinner* saved by grace. And if there is not radical, concrete growth in confidence and joy (even in difficulties), you don't *really* know you are a sinner saved by *grace*.

What must you do if you lack the humility, love, joy, and confidence you need to face the life issues before you? You should not try to move on past the gospel to "more advanced" principles. Rather, you should shake yourself until more of the gospel "coins" drop and more of the fruit of the Spirit comes out. Until you do that, despite your sound doctrine you will be as selfish, scared, oversensitive, insensitive, and undisciplined as everyone else. Those were the attributes characterizing Jonah. If he had known the gospel as deeply as he should have, he wouldn't have reacted with such hostility and superiority toward Nineveh. But the experience in the storm and in the fish brings him back to the foundations, and he rediscovers the wonder of the gospel. When he says, "Salvation is *really* from the Lord!" he wasn't learning something brand new but was rediscovering and realizing more deeply the truth and wonder of the gospel.

If you think you really understand the gospel—you don't. If you think you haven't even begun to truly understand the gospel—you do. As important as our "gospel theologizing" is, it alone will not reach our world. People today are incredibly sensitive to inconsistency and phoniness. They hear what the gospel teaches and then look at our lives and see the gap. Why should they believe? We have to recognize that the gospel is a transforming thing, and we simply are not very transformed by it. It's not enough to say to postmodern people: "You don't like absolute truth? Well, then, we're going to give you even more of it!" But people who balk so much at absolute truth will need to see greater holiness of life, practical grace, gospel character, and virtue, if they are going to believe.

Traditionally, this process of "gospel-realizing," especially when done corporately, is called "revival." Religion operates on the principle: *I obey; therefore I am accepted (by God).* The gospel operates on the principle: *I am accepted through the costly grace of God; therefore I obey.* Two people operating on these two principles can sit beside each other in church on Sunday trying to do many of the same things—read the Bible, obey the Ten Commandments, be active in church, and pray—but out of two entirely different motivations. Religion moves you to do what you do out of fear, insecurity, and self-righteousness, but the gospel moves you to do what you do more and more out of grateful joy in who God is in himself. Times of revival are seasons in which many nominal and spiritually sleepy Christians, operating out of the semi-Pharisaism of religion, wake up to the wonder and ramifications of the gospel. Revivals are massive eruptions of new spiritual power in the church through a recovery of the gospel. In his sermon on Mark 9 Lloyd-Jones was calling the church to revival as its only hope. This is not a new program or something you can implement through a series of steps. It is a matter of wonder. Peter says that the angels always long to look into the gospel; they never tire of it (1 Pet. 1:12). The gospel is *amazing* love. *Amazing* grace.

### Gospel Urbanizing

Three times Jonah is called to go to Nineveh, which God keeps calling "that *great* city" (1:1; 3:2; 4:11). God puts in front of Jonah the size of it. In Jonah 4:11 he says, "Should not I pity Nineveh, that *great* city, in which there are more than 120,000 persons who do not know their right hand from their left . . . ?" God's reasoning is pretty transparent. Big cities are huge stockpiles of spiritually lost people. How can you *not* find yourself drawn to them? I had a friend once who used this ironclad theological argument on me: "The cities are places where there are more people than plants, and the countryside is the place where there are more plants than people. Since God loves people far more than plants, he must love the city more than the countryside." That's exactly the kind of logic God is using on Jonah here.

Christians and churches, of course, need to be wherever there are people! And there is not a Bible verse that says Christians must live in the cities. But, in general, the cities are disproportionately important with respect to culture. That is where the new immigrants come before moving out into society. That is where the poor often congregate. That is where students, artists, and young creatives cluster. As the cities go, so goes society. Yet Christians are under-represented in cities for all sorts of reasons.

Many Christians today ask, "What do we do about a coarsening culture?" Some have turned to politics. Others are reacting against this, saying that "the church simply must be the church" as a witness to the culture, and let the chips fall where they may. James Boice, in his book *Two Cities, Two Loves*, asserts that until Christians are willing to simply live in and work in major cities in at least the same proportions as other groups, we should stop complaining that we are "losing the culture."[12]

While the small town was the ideal for premodern people, and the suburb was the ideal for modern people, the big city is loved by postmodern people with all its diversity, creativity, and unmanageability. We will never reach the postmodern world with the gospel if we don't urbanize the gospel and create urban versions of gospel communities as strong and as well-known as the suburban (i.e., the megachurch). What would those urban communities look like? David Brooks has written about "Bobos" who combined the crass materialism of the bourgeoisie with the moral relativism of the bohemians.[13] I'd propose that urban Christians would be "reverse Bobos," combining not the worst aspects but the best aspects of these two groups. By practicing the biblical gospel in the city they could combine the creativity, love of diversity, and passion for justice (of the old bohemians) with the moral seriousness and family orientation of the bourgeoisie.

## Gospel Communication

As I mentioned above, evangelism in a postmodern context must be much more thorough, progressive, and process-oriented. There are many stages to bring people through who know nothing at all about the gospel and Christianity. Again, we see something of this in the book of Jonah. In Jonah 3:4 we read, "Jonah began to go into the city, going a day's journey. And he called out, 'Yet forty days, and Nineveh shall be overthrown!'" Notice how little is in that message. Jonah is establishing the reality of divine justice and judgment, of human sin and responsibility. But that's all he speaks of. Later, when the Ninevites repent, the king says: "Who knows? God may turn and relent and turn from his fierce anger, so that we may not perish" (3:9). The king isn't even sure if

---

[12]James Montgomery Boice, *Two Cities, Two Loves: Christian Responsibility in a Crumbling Culture* (Downers Grove, IL: InterVarsity Press, 1996), 165ff.
[13]David Brooks, *Bobos In Paradise: The New Upper Class and How They Got There* (New York: Simon & Schuster, 2001).

God offers grace and forgiveness. It is clear that the Ninevites have very little spiritual understanding here. And though some expositors like to talk about the "revival" in Nineveh in response to Jonah's preaching, it seems obvious that they are not yet in any covenant relationship with God. They have not yet been converted. And yet God responds to that: "When God saw what they did, how they turned from their evil way, God relented of the disaster that he had said he would do to them, and he did not do it" (3:10). He doesn't say to them "You are my people; I am your God." There's no saving relationship here—but there is progress! They have one or two very important planks in a biblical worldview, and to God that makes a difference.

At the risk of over-simplification, I'll lay out four stages that people have to go through to come from complete ignorance of the gospel and Christianity to full embrace. I'll call them (1) intelligibility, (2) credibility, (3) plausibility, and (4) intimacy. By "intimacy" I mean leading someone to a personal commitment. The problem with virtually all modern evangelism programs is that they assume listeners come from a Christianized background, and so they very lightly summarize the gospel (often jumping through stages one to three in minutes) and go right to stage "intimacy." But this is no longer sufficient.

"Intelligibility" means to perceive clearly, and I use this word to refer to what Don Carson calls "world-view evangelism." In his essay in *Telling the Truth* Don analyzes Paul's discourse at Athens in Acts 17.[14] Paul spends nearly the whole time on God and his sovereignty, a God-centered philosophy of history, and other basic planks in a biblical view of reality. He mentions Jesus only briefly and then only speaks of his resurrection. Many people consider this a failure to preach the gospel. They believe that every time you preach you *must* tell people that they are sinners going to hell, that Jesus died on the cross for them, and that they need to repent and believe in him. The problem with this is that until people's minds and worldviews have been prepared, they hear you say "sin" and "grace" and even "God" in terms of their own categories. By going too quickly to this overview you guarantee that they will misunderstand what you are saying.

In the early days of Redeemer Presbyterian Church I saw a number

---

[14]D. A. Carson, "Athens Revisited," in *Telling the Truth*, ed. D. A. Carson (Grand Rapids, MI: Zondervan, 2002), 384–98.

of people make decisions for Christ, but in a couple of years, when some desirable sexual partners came along, they simply bailed out of the faith. I was stunned. Then I realized that in our Manhattan culture people believe that truth is simply "what works for me." There is no concept of a Truth (outside the empirical realm) that is real and there no matter what I feel or think. When I taught them that Jesus was the Truth, they understood it through their own categories. There hadn't really been a power-encounter at the worldview level. They hadn't really changed their worldview furniture. When Jesus didn't "work" for them, he was no longer their Truth.

"Credibility" is the area of "defeaters." A defeater is a widely held belief that most people consider common sense but which contradicts some basic Christian teaching.[15] A defeater is a certain belief (belief A), that, since it is true, means another belief (belief B) just *can't* be true on the face of it. An example of a defeater belief now is: "I just can't believe there is only one true religion, one way to God." Notice that is not an argument—it's just an assertion. There is almost no evidence you can muster for the statement. It is really an emotional expression, but it is so widely held and deeply felt that for many—even most people—it automatically means orthodox Christianity can't be true. Now in the older Western culture there were very few defeater beliefs out there. The great majority of people believed the Bible, believed in God and heaven and hell, and so on. In the old "Evangelism Explosion" training, I remember there was an appendix of "Objections," but you were directed not to bring these up unless the person you were talking to brought them up first. You were to focus on getting through the presentation.

But today you must have a good list of the ten to twenty basic defeaters out there and must speak to them constantly in all your communication and preaching. You have to go after them and show people that all their doubts about Christianity are really *alternate faith-assertions*. You have to show them what they are and ask them for as much warrant and support for their assertions as they are asking for yours. For example, you must show someone who says, "I think all religions are equally valid; no one's view of spiritual reality is

---

[15]For more on this, see my article "Defeating Defeater Beliefs: Leading the Secular to Christ" (http://www.redeemer2.com/themovement/issues/2004/oct/deconstructing.html), as well as my forthcoming book, tentatively titled *Doubting Your Doubts* (New York: Penguin-Dutton).

superior to anyone else's," that that statement is *itself* a faith assertion (it can't be proven) and is itself a view on spiritual reality that he or she thinks is superior to the orthodox Christian view. So the speaker is doing the very thing he is forbidding to others. That's not fair! *That* sort of approach is called "presuppositional apologetics."[16] It uncovers the faith assumptions that skeptics smuggle in to their doubts. It will make them begin to think. If you don't do this, people's eyes will just glaze over as you speak. They will tune you out. Nothing you say will sound plausible to them. You can tell them they are sinners and say "the Bible says," but the defeater belief may be deeply embedded in your listeners that the Bible was written by the winners of a power battle with the Gnostic gospel writers, with the result that all your assertions are incredible.

In "Intelligibility" and "Credibility" you are showing listeners the nonnegotiables and angularities of the faith, the truth claims they have to deal with. But in "Plausibility" you enter deeply into their own hopes, beliefs, aspirations, and longings, and you try to connect with them. This is "contextualization," which makes people very nervous in many circles. To some, it sounds like giving people what they want to hear. But contextualization is showing people how the lines of their own lives, the hopes of their own hearts, and the struggles of their own cultures will be resolved in Jesus Christ. David Wells says that contextualization requires

> not merely a practical application of biblical doctrine but a translation of that doctrine into a conceptuality that meshes with the reality of the social structures and patterns of life dominant in our contemporary life. . . .

> Where is the line between involvement and disengagement, acceptance and denial, continuity and discontinuity, being "in" the world and not "of" the world?

> Contextualization is the process through which we find answer to these questions. The Word of God must be related to our own context. . . . The preservation of its identity [= intelligibility and credibility] is neces-

---

[16]For an introduction, see John Frame's *Apologetics to the Glory of God* (Phillipsburg, NJ: P&R, 1994).

sary for Christian belief; its contemporary relevance [= plausibility] is
required if Christians are to be believable.[17]

Here is an example. When I talk to someone who insists that no
one's view on spiritual reality (faith) is superior to others, I always
respond that that *is* a view of spiritual reality and a claim that the world
would be a better place if others adopted it. *Every*one unavoidably has
"exclusive" views. To insist no one should make a truth claim *is* a truth
claim. So the real question is not *Do you think you have the truth?*
(Everybody does.) The real question is: *Which* set of exclusive truth
claims will lead to a humble, peaceful, non-superior attitude toward
people with whom you deeply differ? At the center of the Christian
truth claim is a man on a cross, dying for his enemies, praying for their
forgiveness. Anyone who thinks out the implications of *that* will be led
to love and respect even their opponents.

What am I doing in the above paragraph? I'm taking a major
theme of my secular culture—namely, that we live in a pluralistic society of conflict and diversity, and we need resources for living at peace
with one another—and I'm arguing that the claim of religious relativism is not a solution, because it is an exclusive claim to superiority
masking itself as something else. Instead I am pointing out that Jesus'
dying on the cross best fulfills the yearning of our pluralistic culture for
peace and respect among people of different faiths. This is contextualizing—showing the plausibility of the gospel in terms my culture can
understand. We have to do this today.

Of course there is always a danger of over-contextualizing, but (as
David Wells indicates in the quote above) there is an equal danger of
under-contextualization. If you *over-adapt*, you may buy into the idols
of the new culture. But if you *under-adapt*, you may be buying into the
idols of the older culture. If you are afraid to adapt somewhat to an
over-experiential culture, you may be too attached to an overly rational
culture. So you have to think it out! To stand pat is no way to stay safe
and doctrinally sound. You have to think it out.

---

[17]David F. Wells, "An American Evangelical Theology: The Painful Transition from Theoria to
Praxis," in *Evangelicalism and Modern America,* ed. George M. Marsden (Grand Rapids, MI:
Eerdmans, 1984), 90, 93.

## Gospel Humiliation

I know this heading sounds pretty strong, but I want to get your attention. In Jonah 3:1–2 we read, "Then the word of the LORD came to Jonah the second time, saying, 'Arise, go to Nineveh, that great city, and call out against it the message that I tell you.'" In Sinclair Ferguson's little book on Jonah he comments on the broken, humbled prophet who hears the second call to Nineveh and answers it. He says:

> God intends to bring life out of death. We may well think of this as the principle behind all evangelism. Indeed we may even call it the Jonah principle, as Jesus seems to have done. . . . [I]t is out of Christ's weakness that the sufficiency of his saving power will be born. . . . [So] fruitful evangelism is a result of this death-producing principle. It is when we come to share spiritually—and on occasions physically—in Christ's death (cf. Phil. 3:10) that his power is demonstrated in our weakness and others are drawn to him. This is exactly what was happening to Jonah.[18]

What does this mean? A man recently shared with me how he was trying to talk about his faith with his neighbors, to little avail. But then some major difficulties came into his life, and he began to let his neighbors know how Christ was helping him face them. They were quite interested and moved by this. It was the Jonah principle! As we experience weakness, as we are brought low, Christ's power is more evident in us.

Lloyd-Jones once gave a sermon on Jacob's wrestling with God. In the talk he told a story of a time when he was living in Wales. He was in a gathering of older ministers who were discussing a young minister with remarkable preaching gifts. This man was being acclaimed, and there was real hope that God could use him to renew and revive his church. The ministers were hopeful. But then one of them said to the others: "Well, all well and good, but you know, I don't think he's been humbled yet." And the other ministers looked very grave. And it hit Lloyd-Jones hard (and it hit me hard) that unless something comes into your life that breaks you of your self-righteousness and pride, you may say you believe the gospel of grace but, as we said above, the penny hasn't dropped. You aren't a sign of the gospel yourself. You don't

---

[18]Sinclair B. Ferguson, *Man Overboard* (Wheaton, IL: Tyndale, 1981), 70–71.

have the Jonah principle working in you. You aren't a strength-out-of-weakness person. God will have to bring you low if he is going to use you in evangelism.

At the end of the book of Jonah, God gives Jonah a "gourd" (KJV) that grows a vine and gives him shade, but then a desert wind blasts the vine and ruins it. Jonah becomes disconsolate. John Newton wrote a hymn largely based on this incident.

> *I asked the Lord that I might grow*
> *In faith, and love, and every grace;*
> *Might more of His salvation know,*
> *And seek, more earnestly, His face.*

> *I hoped that in some favored hour,*
> *At once He'd answer my request;*
> *and by His love's constraining pow'r,*
> *Subdue my sins, and give me rest.*

> *Instead of this, He made me feel*
> *The hidden evils of my heart;*
> *And let the angry pow'rs of hell*
> *Assault my soul in every part.*

> *Yea more, with His own hand*
> *He seemed intent to aggravate my woe;*
> *Crossed all the fair designs I schemed,*
> *Blasted my gourds, and laid me low.*

> *"Lord why is this," I trembling cried,*
> *"Wilt thou pursue thy worm to death?"*
> *"'Tis in this way," the Lord replied,*
> *"I answer prayer for grace and faith."*

> *"These inward trials I employ,*
> *From self and pride to set thee free*
> *And break thy schemes of earthly joy,*
> *That thou may'st find thy all in Me."*[19]

---

[19]John Newton, "I Asked the Lord That I Might Grow" (1779).

**Gospel Incarnation**

I believe Jonah is a setup for the amazing letter from God to the exiles
of Babylon in Jeremiah 29. The Jews had been living in their nation-
state in which everyone was a believer, but when they arrive in Babylon
God tells them to move into that pagan city, filled with unbelievers and
uncleanness, and work for its peace and prosperity—its *shalom*. He
challenges them to use their resources to make the city a great place for
everyone—believers and unbelievers—to live. This is not just supposed
to be a calculated thing or a thing of mere duty. He calls them to pray
for it, which is to love it. This was the city that had destroyed their
homeland! Yet that is the call. God outlines a relationship to pagan
culture. His people are neither to *withdraw* from it nor *assimilate* to
it. They are to remain *distinct but engaged*. They are to be different,
but out of that difference they are to sacrificially serve and love the
city where they are exiles. And if their city prospers, then they too will
prosper.

This is really astonishing, but the book of Jonah gets us ready for
all this. Jonah is called to go to a pagan city to help it avoid destruction, but he is too hostile toward them to want to go. He runs away,
but God puts him on a boat filled with pagans anyway. There Jonah is
asleep in the boat during the storm. He is awakened by the sailors, who
tell him to call on his God to ask him to keep the boat from sinking.
They ask him to use his relationship to God to benefit the public good.
The Scottish writer Hugh Martin wrote a commentary on this text and
called this chapter "The World Rebuking the Church."[20] Eventually
Jonah goes to Nineveh—but when God turns away from destroying
them, Jonah is furious. This time God rebukes him for not caring about
the whole city and its welfare. Jonah 4:10–11: "You pity the plant. . . .
Should not *I* pity Nineveh, that great city, in which there are more than
120,000 persons who do not know their right hand from their left, and
also much cattle?"

This is a picture of the church's problem in a postmodern world.
We simply don't like the unwashed pagans. Jonah *went* to the city but
didn't *love* the city. Likewise, we don't love the postmodern world in
the way we should. We disdain these people who don't believe in Truth.
We create our subculture and we invite people to join us inside, but we

---

[20]Hugh Martin, *The Prophet Jonah* (1866; repr., Edinburgh: Banner of Truth, 1978).

don't take our time, gifts, and money and pour ourselves out in deeds of love and service to our city. Does the world recognize our love for them? Are we the kind of church of which the world says: *We don't share a lot of their beliefs, but I shudder to think of this city without them. They are such an important part of the community. They give so much! If they left we'd have to raise taxes because others won't give of themselves like those people do.* "Though they accuse you . . . they . . . see your good deeds and glorify God" (1 Pet. 2:12, NIV; cf. Matt. 5:16).

Where do you get the courage and power to live like that? Well, here. Centuries after Jonah, there was another sleeper in a storm—Jesus Christ (Mark 4). And he was surrounded by his disciples who, like the sailors, were terrified. And in exactly the same way they woke him up and said, "Don't you care? Do something or we will drown!" So Jesus waved his hand, calmed the sea, and everyone was saved. So for all the similarities, the stories of Jonah and Jesus are very different at the end. Whereas Jonah was sacrificed and thrown into the storm of wrath so the sailors could be saved, Jesus wasn't sacrificed. But wait. On the cross, Jesus *was* thrown into the real storm, the ultimate storm. He went under the wrath of God and *was* drowned in order that we could be saved.

Do you see that? If you do, then you have *both* the strength and the weakness, the power and the pattern, to pour yourself out for your city. Ultimately, the gospel is not a set of principles but is Jesus Christ himself. See the supremacy of Christ in the gospel. Look at him, and if you see him bowing his head into that ultimate storm, for us, then we can be what we should be.

### Conclusion

Since we began looking at Mark 9 we should not forget that "this kind" of demon "only comes out through prayer." Lloyd-Jones applies this to the church today by insisting that it needs a comprehensive spiritual transformation if we are going to evangelize our world with the gospel. There's a (probably apocryphal) story about Alexander the Great, who had a general whose daughter was getting married. Alexander valued this soldier greatly and offered to pay for the wedding. When the general gave Alexander's steward the bill, it was absolutely enormous.

The steward came to Alexander and named the sum. To his surprise Alexander smiled and said, "Pay it! Don't you see—by asking me for such an enormous sum he does me great honor. He shows that he believes I am both rich *and* generous."

Are we insulting God by our small ambitions and low expectations for evangelism today?

> *Thou art coming to a King,*
> *Large petitions with thee bring;*
> *For His grace and power are such,*
> *None can ever ask too much.*[21]

---

[21]John Newton, "Come, My Soul, Thy Suit Prepare" (1779).

# CHAPTER 6

# The Church and the Supremacy of Christ in a Postmodern World ·

MARK DRISCOLL

Roughly two thousand years ago, a young virgin woman named Mary gave birth to her firstborn son, Jesus, in a dumpy, rural, hick town, not unlike those today where guys change their own oil on their El Camino, think pro wrestling is real, and drink wine from a box as an essential part of a fancy meal. Jesus was adopted by Mary's husband, Joseph, who was a carpenter. For roughly the first thirty years of his life, Jesus lived in relative obscurity, swinging a hammer with his dad. Then Jesus spent about three years doing public ministry that included preaching to multitudes, healing the sick, feeding the hungry, training his disciples, evangelizing the lost, befriending the outcast, and scrapping with the stuffed-shirt religious types who had taken all the fun out of fundamentalism.

At first glance, Jesus' résumé is rather simple. He never traveled more than a few hundred miles from his home. He never held a political office, never married, never had intimate relations, never wrote a book, never went to college, never visited a big city, and never drove a stick shift. He died both homeless and broke.

Nonetheless, Jesus' legacy is unprecedented; he is the most famous person in all of human history. History, in fact, literally hinges upon his life; our calendar is divided into the years before and after his birth, noted as B.C. ("before Christ") and A.D. (*anno Domini*, meaning "in the year of the Lord"), respectively. More songs have been sung to

Jesus, books written about Jesus, and artwork commissioned of Jesus than anyone who has ever lived.

Jesus has also transcended the world of faith and religion and has emerged as an icon in the world of entertainment and pop culture. In recent years, two of the top-grossing films, *The Passion of the Christ* and *The Da Vinci Code*, were based on the life of Jesus. Additionally, the blockbuster movie *The Chronicles of Narnia* imagined what would happen if Jesus had been incarnated in Narnia, with Aslan as the "Lion of the tribe of Judah"[1] who died and rose to save his people from evil and death. In the film *Talladega Nights: The Ballad of Ricky Bobby*, comedian Will Ferrell (as Ricky Bobby) prays to an "eight-pound, six-ounce, newborn infant Jesus" in "golden, fleece diapers."

In the world of music, even unbelievers such as Kanye West cannot help but sing about Jesus. Joining him is everyone from alternative rockers The Killers to American-Idol-turned-country-music-darling Carrie Underwood.

In the world of fashion, the number of Jesus T-shirts is countless. One of the most popular says, "Jesus is my homeboy." Everyone from Madonna to Pamela Anderson, Ashton Kutcher, Ben Affleck, and Brad Pitt has been seen wearing it.

Every month it seems at least one major magazine has an article about Jesus on its cover. A few years back, for example, the typically nap-worthy, staid magazine *Popular Mechanics* ran a cover story about their quest for the real face of Jesus.[2]

On television, Jesus often appears on the long-running animation hits *The Simpsons* and *South Park*. Jesus also appears in the comedic sketches of vulgar comic Carlos Mencia's hit show *Mind of Mencia*. Dog the Bounty Hunter prays to Jesus on almost every episode of his hit television show.

Even the cross, which represents Jesus' torturous death, has become the most famous and popular symbol in all of history. In 2006, Madonna concluded each concert during her $193 million-grossing Confessions tour by being laid upon a disco cross. Also in 2006, both old-school rocker Axl Rose of Guns N' Roses and bullet-ridden rapper 50 Cent wore crosses around their necks to the MTV Video Music Awards.

---

[1] Rev. 5:5.
[2] Mike Fillon, "The Real Face of Jesus," *Popular Mechanics*, December 2002, http://www.popular-mechanics.com/science/research/1282186.html.

In short, Jesus is as popular, controversial, and misunderstood as ever. Therefore, it is imperative that Christians contend for a faithful and biblical Christology and contextualize that Christology for a fruitful and cultural missiology.

## The Supremacy of Christ in a Postmodern World

The September 2006 cover story of *Christianity Today* announced the resurgence of Reformed theology among younger evangelical leaders.[3] The article also noted that competing with Reformed theology in popularity is Emergent theology, perhaps most identified with Brian McLaren and Rob Bell.[4] According to the article, Emergent theology has been overtaken in popularity by cool Calvinism. Without wanting to be reductionistic, from my vantage point (as someone who was an early leader in Emergent circles but had to distance himself theologically from that tribe because of his evangelical and Reformed convictions, while still maintaining sincere friendships with some of the leaders), much of the debate between these two tribes results from a conflict of Christologies.

Over the centuries, various Christian traditions have been prone to emphasize either the incarnation/humanity of Jesus or the exaltation/divinity of Jesus at the expense of the other. Liberals and their Emergent offspring generally prefer the former, while conservatives and fundamentalists generally prefer the latter. On this matter we must be careful to avoid reductionism whereby we embrace only part of the truth and in so doing undermine it altogether.

It was the Council of Chalcedon in A.D. 451 that helped to clarify what Scripture says on this matter of Christology. They issued the Chalcedonian Creed, which declared that Jesus Christ is one person with two natures (human and divine) who is both fully God and fully man. Theologically, the term for the union of both natures in Jesus Christ is *hypostatic union*. The Chalcedonian summary of the incarnation is the position held by all of Christendom, including Orthodox, Catholic, and Protestant Christians, despite numerous differences they have on various other matters.

---

[3]Collin Hansen, "Young, Restless, Reformed," *Christianity Today* (September 2006), http://www.christianitytoday.com/ct/2006/september/42.32.html. Hansen's forthcoming book will explore the resurgence in greater detail.
[4]See www.emergentvillage.com.

*Incarnation*

One of the reasons many Christians are drawn to Emergent thinking is because of its emphasis on the incarnation and subsequent humanity of Jesus Christ, as stressed in such places as the Gospels (especially Luke) and Philippians 2:1–11. An incarnational Christology is attractive in that it stresses the immanence of God at work here with us. It focuses on bringing about the new way of life offered to the citizens of the kingdom of God. Furthermore, this incarnational Christology paves the way for a robust missiology, which is the wonderful upside of a rigorous understanding of the incarnation of Jesus Christ.

As the second member of the Trinity, Jesus Christ ruled from eternity past as God exalted in glory. He then humbly entered into history as a man to identify with us. The common jargon for the second member of the Trinity entering into history as a human being is *incarnation* (from the Latin meaning "becoming flesh"); it is a biblical concept.[5]

On the earth, Jesus grew from infancy to adulthood, had a family, worked a job, ate meals, increased his knowledge through learning, told jokes, attended funerals, had male and female friends, celebrated holidays, went to parties, loved his parents, felt the pain of betrayal and lies told about him, and experienced the full range of human emotions from stress to astonishment, joy, compassion, and sorrow. Furthermore, Jesus experienced the same sorts of trials and temptations that we do,[6] with the exception that he never sinned.[7] Subsequently, Jesus lived the sinless life that we are supposed to live but have not; he was both our substitute and our example.

Significantly, Jesus lived his sinless life on the earth in large part by the power of the Holy Spirit. This does not mean that Jesus in any way ceased to be fully God while on the earth, but rather as Philippians 2:5–11 shows, he humbly chose not always to avail himself of his divine attributes. Thus, he often lived as we must live: by the enabling power of God the Holy Spirit. I want to be clear: Jesus remained fully God during his incarnation while also fully man on the earth; he maintained all of his divine attributes and availed himself of them upon occasion, such as to forgive human sin, which God alone can do.[8] Nonetheless,

---

[5]John 1:14; Phil. 2:5–6; Col. 2:9; 1 John 4:2
[6]For example, Matt. 4:1–10; Heb. 4:14–16
[7]John 8:46; 2 Cor. 5:21; Heb. 4:14–16; 1 Pet. 1:19
[8]Mark 2:1–7

Jesus' life was lived as fully human in that he lived by the power of the Holy Spirit.

This point is perhaps best witnessed in the writings of Luke. The empowerment of Jesus through God the Holy Spirit is repeatedly stressed in his Gospel. There we find that Jesus was conceived by the Holy Spirit and given the title "Christ," which means anointed by the Holy Spirit.[9] Jesus baptized people with the Holy Spirit,[10] and the Holy Spirit descended upon Jesus at his own baptism.[11] Furthermore, Jesus was "full of the Holy Spirit" and "led by the Spirit,"[12] came "in the power of the Spirit,"[13] and declared that "the Spirit of the Lord is upon me."[14] He also "rejoiced in the Holy Spirit."[15] Regarding the Holy Spirit's ministry to and through Christians, Jesus also promised that God the Father would "give the Holy Spirit to those who ask him"[16] and that the Holy Spirit would teach us once he was sent.[17]

In Luke's sequel, the book of Acts, Jesus told his followers to wait for the coming Holy Spirit to empower them for life and ministry, just before ascending back into heaven.[18] Then the Holy Spirit descended upon the early Christians just as he had descended upon Jesus.[19] In this way, God revealed that through the power of the Holy Spirit, the followers of Jesus are given the ability to live a life like Jesus (though admittedly imperfectly since we remain sinners) by the same Holy Spirit that enabled Jesus. The result of the arrival of the Holy Spirit is that throughout the book of Acts, God's people are missionally engaged in culture, just as Jesus was.

Practically, Luke's revelation of Jesus' continual reliance upon God the Holy Spirit is important because it allows us to see that Jesus really was tempted as a missionary in culture. Jesus really did suffer like us and really did triumph, as we also can by the power of the Spirit. Sadly, without an acknowledgement of the full humanity of Jesus, we are left with a Jesus who appears eerily similar to Superman. We are

---

[9]Luke 1–2
[10]Luke 3:16
[11]Luke 3:21–22
[12]Luke 4:1–2
[13]Luke 4:14
[14]Luke 4:18; cf. Isa. 61:1
[15]Luke 10:21
[16]Luke 11:13
[17]Luke 12:12
[18]Acts 1
[19]Acts 2

left to believe that although Jesus looked like a Galilean carpenter, he did not really endure temptation and suffering as we do. The deity of Jesus without the humanity of Jesus tragically leaves us to see Jesus as a faker, not unlike Clark Kent. All we are left with is someone who cannot really sympathize with us in our weakness, as Hebrews says,[20] because he was not fully human.

All of this matters because Jesus' life was the perfect human life of a missionary in culture. He lived the life that we are each supposed to live as missionaries in culture; we can therefore pattern our lives after his by the power of God the Holy Spirit. However, there has been a tendency in some theological circles to virtually ignore the humanity of Jesus and the details of his life on the earth in culture. For example, the Apostles' Creed says that Jesus "was conceived by the Holy Spirit, born of the Virgin Mary, suffered under Pontius Pilate, was crucified, dead, and buried." Curiously, this creed essentially says nothing about Jesus' life as a man on the earth. Instead, it moves quickly from his birth to his death without any mention of his life in culture.

Fortunately, what is being recovered along with a vibrant incarnational Christology is a robust missiology. Jesus came to earth and entered into a sinful culture as a missionary. Therefore, not only is Jesus our prophet who speaks to us, our priest who heals us, and our king who rules over us, but he is also the model missionary who leads us into culture, enabled by the Holy Spirit and equipped with the truth of the gospel so that others may be saved from their sin by trusting in Jesus Christ.

In conclusion, the Emergent connection of the humble incarnation of Jesus into culture as our missional model is a glorious rediscovery of a biblical truth. It is inspiring a generation of young Christians not merely to sign up for mission trips around the globe, but also to move into neighborhoods in their own city to live in community with lost people as missionaries like Jesus himself modeled. The result has been a refreshing interest in everything from living in Christian community in urban centers to various forms of church planting intended to reach new cultures and subcultures of people who do not connect with more traditional churches.

However, as is often the case, the strength is also the weakness. By

---

[20]Heb. 4:15

itself, an incarnational Christology, though true, is not truly complete. Without a robust recognition of the corresponding deity of Jesus, the humanity of Jesus has the propensity to leave us with a marred false image of Jesus—little more than a limp-wristed, marginalized, hippie-esque, unemployed Galilean pacifist in a dress with feathered hair and open-toed sandals—a guy that the average man would be remiss to worship because he could beat up that Jesus. Therefore, in addition to the humble incarnation of Jesus where his humanity shines forth, we must also retain the glorious exaltation of Jesus where his divinity likewise shines forth. While it is the Emergent tribe of Christians that has perhaps most zealously explored the humble incarnation of Jesus the man, it is the Reformed tribe of Christians that has most ardently defended the glorious exaltation of Jesus the God-man.

## Exaltation

If we were to see Jesus today, we would not see him in his state of humble incarnation. Rather, we would see Jesus as both Isaiah and John saw him[21]—enthroned in glory as King of kings and Lord of lords. This Jesus rules over gays and straights, men and women, young and old, rich and poor, black and white, simple and wise, healthy and sick, powerful and powerless, Republicans and Democrats, married and single, Christians and non-Christians, angels and demons, and the living and the dead.

The sovereign, unprecedented, and glorious exaltation of Jesus is typified by a throne. The imagery of a throne is used roughly 196 times in Scripture, with 135 occurrences in the Old Testament and 61 occurrences in the New Testament. Of the New Testament occurrences, 45 of the 61 are in the book of Revelation. The imagery of the throne appears in seventeen of its twenty-two chapters. The book of Revelation breaks into earthly scenes of sin and the curse, as well as heavenly scenes of worship and rule. The central piece of furniture on the stage of the heavenly scenes is the throne. Seated upon the throne over all peoples, times, places, and cultures is Jesus Christ. Throughout Revelation, all truth, authority, and judgment proceed from the One seated on the throne. All praise, worship, and gladness proceed to the One seated

---

[21]Isa. 6:1–5; John 12:41

on the throne from all created beings, including men, women, angels, beasts of the field, birds of the air, and fish of the sea.

Perhaps my favorite picture (and that of my young sons) of the glorious exaltation of our great God Jesus Christ is what we like to refer to as Ultimate Fighter Jesus. In Revelation 19:11–16, Jesus rides into town on a white horse, with his steely eyes blazing red like fire and a tattoo down his leg that says "King of kings and Lord of lords." He is wearing white like a gunslinger from an old western and carrying a sword, looking for some bad guys as the blood of already-fallen enemies drips to the ground below. Simply, Jesus was, is, and forever will be fully God; he is not someone anyone would want to mess with.

The supremacy of Jesus Christ as our sovereign and exalted God is our authority for mission. There is not one inch of creation, one culture or subculture of people, one lifestyle or orientation, one religion or philosophical system, that he does not possess full authority over and command to turn from sin and glorify him.[22] We derive our authority to preach the gospel to all peoples, times, and places from the glorious exaltation of our great God and Savior Jesus Christ. Jesus claimed all authority for himself and commanded us to go in his authority to preach the gospel truth: "that Christ died for our sins in accordance with the Scriptures, that he was buried, that he was raised on the third day in accordance with the Scriptures."[23] Jesus himself said, "All authority in heaven and on earth has been given to me. Go therefore and make disciples of all nations, baptizing them in the name of the Father and of the Son and of the Holy Spirit, teaching them to observe all that I have commanded you. And behold, I am with you always, to the end of the age."[24] Indeed, the authority of our mission rests on nothing less than the authority delegated to us by the exalted Lord Jesus Christ who rules over all.

Nevertheless, as Christians enter into their local culture and its subcultures, we must also remember that it is Jesus (not us) who is sovereign, and it is Jesus (not the church) who rules over all. We are to come in the authority of the exalted Jesus, but also in the example of the humble incarnated Jesus. This means that we must come into cul-

---

[22]As Abraham Kuyper says: "There is not a square inch in the whole domain of our human existence over which Christ, who is Sovereign over all, does not cry, 'Mine!'" Abraham Kuyper, *Abraham Kuyper: A Centennial Reader*, ed. James D. Bratt (Grand Rapids, MI: Eerdmans, 1998), 488.
[23]1 Cor. 15:3–4
[24]Matt. 28:18–20

ture as Jesus did—filled with the Holy Spirit, in constant prayer to the Father, saturated with the truth of Scripture, humble in our approach, loving in our truth, and serving in our deeds. Once we have the incarnation and exaltation clear in our Christology, we are then sufficiently ready to contend for the truth of the gospel and contextualize it rightly for various cultures and subcultures of people, as Jesus did and commands us to do.

### The Role of the Church in a Postmodern World

Not only must God's people personally believe the gospel of Jesus Christ, but they also must publicly contend for it. This is because the gospel is under continual attack by Satan, the "father of lies,"[25] and a seemingly endless army of false teachers, false prophets, false shepherds, and false apostles, whom he sends to wage war against the church. The New Testament letters model a warrior's battle cry, declaring that heretics are: dogs and evildoers,[26] empty and deceitful,[27] puffed up without reason,[28] given to mythical speculation and vanity without understanding,[29] products of a shipwrecked faith,[30] demonic liars with seared consciences,[31] peddlers of silly myths,[32] arrogant fools with depraved minds,[33] the spiritual equivalent of gangrene,[34] foolish and ignorant,[35] chatty deceivers,[36] destructive blasphemers,[37] ignorantly unstable,[38] and antichrists.[39]

In our day of pluralistic, postmodern, perspectival politeness, the terse language of Peter and Paul seems narrowly intolerant, as if they had never been enlightened by taking a philosophy of religion class at a community college from a long-haired, self-medicated grad student. Nonetheless, the truth is the truth, and Peter, Paul, and many of the

---

[25]John 8:44
[26]Phil. 3:2
[27]Col. 2:8
[28]Col. 2:18
[29]1 Tim. 1:3–7
[30]1 Tim. 1:19
[31]1 Tim. 4:1–2
[32]1 Tim. 4:7
[33]1 Tim. 6:3–5
[34]2 Tim. 2:14–18
[35]2 Tim. 2:23
[36]Titus 1:10–14
[37]2 Pet. 2:1–3
[38]2 Pet. 3:16
[39]1 John 2:18

faithful who have followed Jesus on the narrow road of truth have seen their blood spilled by those who were as brotherly as Cain for contending for the truth.

### Contending

Since nothing short of God's glory and human eternal destiny are at stake when it comes to matters of the truth, we must contend for it like Jude 3 commands: "Beloved, although I was very eager to write to you about our common salvation, I found it necessary to write appealing to you to *contend* for the faith that was once for all delivered to the saints." In every age there are certain doctrines that are attacked in varying ways by the occasional "innovative" wingnut. In our day there are many, but for the sake of brevity I will only list ten theological issues we must contend for, not necessarily in order of importance. There is much more that can and should be said about each point.

1) *Scripture as inerrant, timeless truth.* In the opening pages of Genesis, we see that one of the Serpent's first tricks was hermeneutical in nature. While he did not seek to take God's Word away from our first parents, Adam and Eve, the Serpent instead sought to change the meaning of what God had said. Sadly, the Serpent has been up to his old tricks ever since.

The new serpentine hermeneutic goes by many names, including *trajectory hermeneutic* and *redemptive-arc hermeneutic.* Perhaps the most popular preacher in America using this approach to Scripture is Rob Bell. In his book *Velvet Elvis,* Bell calls the doctrines of the Christian faith "springs," not "bricks," and encourages his readers to challenge and question Christian doctrines (like the virgin birth and the Trinity) so that they stretch like springs.[40] He also says that verses in the Bible "aren't first and foremost timeless truths."[41]

Brian McLaren also says that the Bible is "not a look-it-up encyclopedia of timeless moral truths."[42] Nonetheless, at the Society of Biblical Literature's 2006 annual meeting, Phyllis Tickle, author of two dozen books on religion and spirituality who often appears as an expert on the subjects in *Publishers Weekly, USA Today, The New York Times,*

---

[40]Rob Bell, *Velvet Elvis: Repainting the Christian Faith* (Grand Rapids, MI: Zondervan, 2006), 21–27.
[41]Ibid., 62.
[42]Brian D. McLaren, A *Generous Orthodoxy* (Grand Rapids, MI: Zondervan, 2004), 171.

PBS, and NPR, said that "Brian McLaren is to this new reformation what Martin Luther was to the Protestant Reformation."[43]

While it is true that the truths of Scripture did not arrive apart from a context and culture, we must affirm that these truths still have application for today. Few have said it better than D. A. Carson: "No truth which human beings may articulate can ever be articulated in a culture-transcending way—but that does not mean that the truth thus articulated does not transcend culture."[44]

Because Scripture reveals to us the person and work of Jesus and is the way in which God has chosen to speak to all people, we must contend for the inerrant perfection and cross-cultural authority of all Scripture as timeless truth.

2) *The sovereignty and foreknowledge of God.* In recent years, a view of God contrary to classic Protestant theism has gained popularity in some circles. It goes by various names, such as *an open view of God, openness theology,* and *open theism.* It undermines the biblical teaching that God is both fully sovereign over and knowledgeable of the future.

Because open theism undermines who God has revealed himself to be in Scripture,[45] we must contend for both the sovereignty and foreknowledge of God.

3) *The virgin birth of Jesus.* Perhaps the most curious doctrine to be undermined recently is the virgin birth of Jesus Christ. Bell says that if the virgin birth of Jesus was taken away from our faith and we instead learned that "Jesus had a real, earthly, biological father named Larry, and archaeologists find Larry's tomb and do DNA samples and prove beyond a shadow of a doubt that the virgin birth was really just a bit of mythologizing the Gospel writers threw in to appeal to the followers of the Mithra and Dionysian religious cults that were hugely popular at the time," we would essentially not lose any significant part of our faith because it is more about how we live.[46]

---

[43]Adam Walker Cleaveland, blog entry "SBL/AAR Day 2/3 & What is Emergent?" Pomomusings Blog, posted November 20, 2006, http://pomomusings.com/2006/11/20/sblaar-day-23-what-is-emergent/ (accessed February 15, 2007).

[44]D. A. Carson, "Maintaining Scientific and Christian Truths in a Postmodern World," *Science & Christian Belief,* vol. 14, no. 2 (October 2002): 107–22, http://www.scienceandchristianbelief.org/articles/carson.pdf.

[45]Ps. 139:1–16; Isa. 37:26; 46:8–11; Eph. 1:4–5; Acts 2:23; 4:24–28; 8:28–30; 11:2; Rom. 9:14–24; Rev. 1:8

[46]Bell, *Velvet Elvis,* 26.

The only alternative to the virgin birth offered in Scripture is that Mary was a sexually sinful woman who conceived Jesus illegitimately, which was the accusation in Jesus' day.[47] If the virgin birth of Jesus is untrue, then the story of Jesus changes greatly; we would have a sexually promiscuous young woman lying about God's miraculous hand in the birth of her son, raising that son to declare he was God, and then joining his religion.[48] But if Mary is nothing more than a sinful con artist then neither she nor her son Jesus should be trusted.

Because both the clear teachings of Scripture about the beginning of Jesus' earthly life and the character of his mother are at stake, we must contend for the virgin birth of Jesus Christ.

4) *Our sin nature and total depravity.* It seems that every age has a groundswell of support for the denial of the doctrines of original sin and total depravity, despite overwhelming evidence that anyone awake long enough to actually see the world could hardly deny. In the early church a debate arose between Augustine, who argued that we are all sinners by nature, and Pelagius, who denied that we are by nature inherently sinful. Pelagius was ultimately condemned as a heretic at the Council of Carthage (A.D. 418). Nonetheless, one of the founders of the Emergent community, Doug Pagitt, has defended the theology of Pelagius. He argues that Pelagius was excommunicated from the church "on false pretenses and for personal and political and not primarily doctrinal reasons."[49]

Because God is holy, we are sinners, and Jesus' mission was to save sinners, we must contend for the truth that we are totally depraved sinners by nature and choice.[50]

5) *Jesus' death as our penal substitution.* The doctrine of penal substitutionary atonement is regarded by many as the primary accomplishment of Jesus' death on the cross, in addition to innumerable secondary accomplishments. Publishers such as InterVarsity Press have ironically published some of the greatest books on the cross of Jesus[51] and some

---

[47]Matt. 13:55; Mark 6:3; John 8:41

[48]Acts 1:14

[49]Doug Pagitt, "The Emerging Church and Embodied Theology," in *Listening to the Beliefs of Emerging Churches*, ed. Robert Webber (Grand Rapids, MI: Zondervan, 2007), 128.

[50]Rom. 3:23; see also Ps. 53:3; Isa. 53:6; 64:6; 1 John 1:18

[51]For example, John Stott's *The Cross of Christ* and Leon Morris's *The Atonement*. I also recommend the forthcoming book *Pierced for Our Transgressions: Rediscovering the Glory of Penal Substitution* by Steve Jeffery, Michael Ovey, and Andrew Sach (Wheaton, IL: Crossway Books, 2007).

of the worst books on the cross of Jesus. Perhaps the very worst of the worst offers a crude caricature of the doctrine of penal substitution: "God takes on the role of the sadist inflicting punishment, while Jesus, in his role as masochist, readily embraces suffering."[52] The authors say that penal substitution "has been understood in ways that have proven detrimental to the witness of the church."[53] They conclude that "it will not do, therefore, to characterize the atonement as God's punishment falling on Christ."[54] This sort of understanding is favored by men such as Brian McLaren, who recommends the previously quoted book.[55]

Another book suggests that we should throw out the atonement because people today do not believe they are sinners: "In an increasingly 'sinless' society, where guilt is a marginal concern, even such functional views of the atonement are wholly inadequate in expressing the actuality of the atonement."[56] The author goes on to say that "a meaningful and appropriate story of atonement must be one that speaks dynamically and specifically to the plight of the post-industrialized, 'sinless' self as the self perceives it, and not as we would wish to describe it."[57]

Because the gospel is at stake, we must contend that Jesus was wounded and crushed for our sins[58] and died for us[59] and our sins[60] by bearing our sins on the cross[61] as our substitute.

6) *Jesus' exclusivity as the only possible means of salvation.* Oprah Winfrey expressed the thoughts of many in our age of spiritual pluralism, saying, "One of the biggest mistakes humans make is to believe there is only one way. Actually, there are many diverse paths leading to what you call God."[62] While the view seems kind and generously open

---

[52]Joel B. Green and Mark D. Baker, *Recovering the Scandal of the Cross* (Downers Grove, IL: InterVarsity Press, 2000), 30.

[53]Ibid., 32.

[54]Ibid., 113.

[55]McLaren, *Generous Orthodoxy*, 47 n. 17. McLaren also endorsed a book that refers to the doctrine of penal substitutionary atonement as "cosmic child abuse." In fact, McLaren said that this book "could help save Jesus from Christianity." Steve Chalke and Alan Mann, *The Lost Message of Jesus* (Grand Rapids, MI: Zondervan, 2003), 182–83.

[56]Alan Mann, *Atonement for a 'Sinless' Society* (Carlisle: Paternoster, 2005), 47.

[57]Ibid., 53–54. In his endorsement for this book, McLaren said, "The first time I heard that devout and thoughtful Christians were questioning conventional understandings of atonement, I was shocked and concerned. As I explored further, I became convinced that this rethinking is essential. . . ."

[58]Isa. 53:5–6

[59]Rom. 5:8

[60]1 Cor. 15:3

[61]1 Pet. 2:24; 3:18

[62]Cited in LaTonya Taylor, "The Church of O," *Christianity Today*, vol. 46, no. 4 (April 1, 2002): 38.

to all faiths, the belief is as foolish as saying that every road one might travel in his life ultimately leads to the same destination.

Because the superiority, glory, exclusivity, preeminence, and singularity of Jesus as both God and Savior are at stake, we must contend for Jesus as the only God and the only possible means of salvation, as both Jesus[63] and the early church[64] did.

7) *God-designed complementary male and female gender distinctions.* Evangelical feminism has become widely popular today as it seeks to eradicate the gender distinctions and roles that God assigns to us in the church and home. The result is an increase in female pastors in the church and a lack of loving masculine leadership in the home. Going one step further is an effort to refer to God as someone other than Father and to Jesus as someone other than a male. Going even further is the attempt by some to eradicate our created gender distinctions so that homosexuality is no longer considered an aberrant and sinful lifestyle.

Because the health and faithfulness of both the home and church are at stake, our God-designed male and female gender distinctions must be contended for against both feminism and homosexuality.

8) *The conscious eternal torments of hell.* Today there are some notable Christian leaders who have sought to redefine the hellishness of hell. Perhaps the most prominent is Brian McLaren in his book *The Last Word and the Word After That.*[65] On September 2, 2006, the issue of hell made the front page of the *Los Angeles Times* in a lengthy article.[66] It explained a falling out of sorts between notable pastor Chuck Smith Sr., leader of the Calvary Chapel movement with some one thousand churches in the United States alone, and his son and namesake, Chuck Smith Jr., over a number of theological issues. On the issue of hell, the article said, "For years, Smith Jr. said, he had preached about hell uncomfortably, half-apologetically, because he couldn't understand why a loving God would consign his children to eternal flames. It felt like blackmail for a pastor to threaten people with hell-scapes from the Middle Ages to induce piety. Now, he came to believe that the biblical images used to depict hell's torments—such

---

[63]John 14:6

[64]Acts 4:12

[65]Brian D. McLaren, *The Last Word and the Word After That* (San Francisco: Jossey-Bass, 2005).

[66]Christopher Goffard, "Father, Son and Holy Rift," *Los Angeles Times* (September 2, 2006).

as the 'lake of fire' and the 'worm that does not die'—were intended to evoke a feeling rather than a literal place."[67]

Because God is holy, we are sinful, justice is beautiful, and God will not be mocked, we must contend for the conscious, eternal torments of hell and invite everyone to avoid its clutches by turning from sin to Jesus, who speaks of hell more than anyone in Scripture.

9) *The preeminence of God's kingdom over human culture.* Due to the postmodern fascination with the present, there is a growing interest in the immediacy of the kingdom of God. For example, it is increasingly argued that the eschatological timeline of the New Testament ended with the Jewish age and the destruction of the temple (A.D. 70), and not the end of the world, as we have wrongly understood it.[68] But such a misunderstanding is actually quite old. The church at Corinth suffered from a similar overrealized eschatology, which led to a laundry list of sins and errors. The same are plaguing many churches today, such as addiction to philosophy, sexual sin of every sort and kind, alcohol abuse, gender confusion, homosexuality, and a denial of the need for a resurrection to enter the kingdom of God.

Because the postmodern fascination with the present leads to the same sort of cultural worldliness as is rebuked in Paul's letters to the Corinthians, we must contend that there is an eternal state marked by God's kingdom that takes preeminence over any culture and its faddish trends in defining faithful Christianity.

10) *The recognition that Satan and demons are real and at work in the world.* As Paul says in the closing chapter of Ephesians, behind all of the philosophical, gender, and lifestyle wars is an even more insidious battle being waged by Satan and demons against God's people and God's truth. Because spiritual warfare has real consequences, we must prayerfully contend that Satan and demons are real and at work in the world today as they always have been.

*Contextualizing*

Once we have rightly understood both the incarnation and exaltation of Jesus Christ and have contended for them both, along with related

---

[67]Ibid.

[68]Andrew Perriman, *The Coming of the Son of Man: New Testament Eschatology for an Emerging Church* (Carlisle: Paternoster, 2006).

truths, we are then ready to contextualize Christian belief and practice to varying cultures and subcultures.

As we examined, in John's Gospel alone, Jesus told us no less than thirty-nine times that he was a missionary from heaven who came to minister incarnationally in an earthly culture.[69] Furthermore, Jesus also commanded us to be missionaries in culture as he was: "As you sent me into the world, so I have sent them into the world."[70] He also said, "As the Father has sent me, even so I am sending you."[71] The Father sent Jesus into a specific time and culture as our example. Therefore, when the incarnation of Jesus is not fully understood, neither is the truth that God in his sovereignty has determined when we would be born and where we would live.[72] He has put every Christian in a time and place as a missionary to bring the good news of Jesus to the people in that culture (in addition to calling some Christians to move from their native culture to a cross-cultural missions situation).

To do that we must follow the example of Jesus; he came into a culture and participated in it fully by using a language, participating in various holidays, eating certain foods, enjoying various drinks, attending parties, befriending people—while never crossing a line into sin. We are to emulate Jesus' perfect and model missionary life lived for God in culture, without falling into the pitfall of liberal syncretism or fundamental sectarianism. It deserves to be noted, however, that for those in the first century who were fundamental and separatistic in their thinking, Jesus simply went too far. In their eyes, though not the eyes of God the Father, his actions were sinful and they falsely accused him of being a glutton, a binge drinker, and a good tipper at Hooters.[73] In reality, in his magnificent High Priestly Prayer, Jesus prayed against us either becoming liberals who go too far into culture and act worldly, or fundamentalists who do not go far enough into culture and act pharisaically: "I do not ask that you take them out of the world, but that you keep them from the evil one. They are not of the world, just as I am not of the world. Sanctify them

---

[69]John 3:34; 4:34; 5:23, 24, 30, 36, 37, 38; 6:29, 38, 39, 44, 57; 7:16, 28, 29, 33; 8:16, 18, 26, 29, 42; 9:4; 10:36; 11:42; 12:44, 45, 49; 13:20; 14:24; 15:21; 16:5; 17:3, 8, 18, 21, 23, 25; 20:21
[70]John 17:18
[71]John 20:21
[72]Acts 17:26
[73]Matt. 11:19

in the truth; your word is truth. As you sent me into the world, so I have sent them into the world."[74]

Jesus prayed that we would not leave the sick and dying world and huddle into a safe subcultural ghetto of Christian nicety, but that we would stay in the world. In the same way, Jesus himself did not remain in the comforts of heaven but rather entered into a sinful culture on the earth as a missionary. Jesus also prayed that we would not simply go with the flow of sin and death in the culture but rather swim upstream against the current of worldliness. We can live countercultural lives like him by being guided by the timeless truths of Scripture that are intended to be lived out by missionaries in every culture.

The undeniable truth is that contextualization is not done just by Christian missionaries in other nations, but it is done by every Christian in every culture—whether they recognize it or not. For example, having the Bible in English rather than the original languages, gathering for church in a building instead of under a tree, choosing to sit rather than stand for the service, choosing to start on time rather than wait for everyone to arrive, watching a pastor in a suit stand behind a pulpit on a platform rather than sitting cross-legged on a floor in a loincloth, and choosing which music we will sing and what (if any) instruments will accompany the singing—all of these are examples of contextualizing Christian faith to a culture. While some may protest that Christian faith and worship do not need to be contexualized to America, they are foolishly overlooking that they have already done it. They assume that their contextualization should work for everyone, as if our pluralistic and multicultural nation is somehow homogenous. We are a nation of numerous languages, races, cultures, subcultures, and styles, with tribes of every sort and kind, and Jesus commands that we as missionaries bring good news to each.

In addition to the incarnational example of Jesus, perhaps the person in Scripture who most exemplifies the missional ministry of contextualizing Christianity for varying culture groups is Paul. Paul's clearest articulation of contextualization is found in 1 Corinthians 9:19–23:

> For though I am free from all, I have made myself a servant to all, that I might win more of them. To the Jews I became as a Jew, in order to win

---

[74]John 17:15–18

Jews. To those under the law I became as one under the law (though not being myself under the law) that I might win those under the law. To those outside the law I became as one outside the law (not being outside the law of God but under the law of Christ) that I might win those outside the law. To the weak I became weak, that I might win the weak. I have become all things to all people, that by all means I might save some. I do it all for the sake of the gospel, that I may share with them in its blessings.

Paul is emphatic that contextualization is nothing short of a gospel issue. It is not a secondary matter to be reserved only for trained missionaries living in foreign lands. If we truly believe the gospel of Jesus, then we should yearn for everyone to hear its truthfulness and see its helpfulness in the most effective manner possible. Therefore, every Christian leader, Christian church, and Christian person must ask themselves if they are doing all that they can to "win more of them . . . for the sake of the gospel."

This is the burning of my heart as a pastor in Seattle. I did not know the gospel until I was nineteen years old, and to this day I have spent more than half of my life utterly lost. I minister in my hometown, which is among the least churched in the nation. In our city there are more dogs than evangelical Christians. Some researchers have even told me that the true percentage of evangelicals in our city is roughly the same as in communist China. Many urban centers across our nation are in the same sad state, which means we must, by God's grace, do all we can to "win more of them . . . for the sake of the gospel." By God's grace, what began as a Bible study in my rental home ten years ago has become a church of more than five thousand people, of which roughly 40 percent were previously unchurched, as far as we are able to verify.

Tragically, my personal experience is that the more conservative and theologically minded a pastor is, the less likely he and his church are to be missionally minded and evangelistically engaged with the people who surround them. This was made painfully clear to me at a meeting I was honored to attend with some of the most able, godly, and skilled Christian preachers I am aware of in our entire nation. As we each took a moment to briefly introduce ourselves and our ministries, nearly every pastor said that everything was going well at his church, with the notable exception that he was not seeing people becoming Christians. Researcher Thom Rainer confirms this fact, saying, "Church leaders are becoming less evangelistic. A survey of pastors I led in 2005 surprised the research team. Over one-half (53 percent) of pastors have made no evangelistic efforts at all in the past six months. They have not shared the Gospel. They have not attempted to engage a lost and unchurched person at any level."[75]

This cannot be seen as anything less than a sin to be repented of. Such repentance requires missiology, the precursor to evangelism. *Missiology* is getting to know a person and his or her culture; in turn, the gospel can be contextualized to that person or people group, which is *evangelism*. The problem is that when we undertake evangelism without conducting a prior missiological study of the culture or without practicing contexualization of the gospel, we do not bear much fruit. Rather, we are communicating in a way that is foreign to the hearer's understanding. By way of analogy, we cannot bear much fruit if we don't first take time to investigate the soil into which the seed of the gospel is to be planted.

### A Two-handed Approach to Christian Ministry

What I am arguing for is a two-handed approach to Christian ministry. In our firmly closed hand we must hold the timeless truths of Christianity, such as the *solas* of the Reformation. In our graciously open hand we must hold timely ministry methods and styles that adapt as the cultures and subcultures we are ministering to change. Practically, this means churches must continually ask questions about their use of technology (e.g., web sites, MP3s, podcasts, e-mails), musical style, dress, verbiage, building aesthetics, programming, and the like: *Are they being as creative, hospitable, relevant, and effective as possible to welcome as many people as possible to connect with Jesus and his church?*

I am not arguing for *relativism,* by which truth is abandoned and all of life and doctrine is lived out of an open hand. Rather, I am arguing for *relevantism,* by which doctrinal principles remain in a closed hand and cultural methods remain in an open hand.

---

[75]Thom S. Rainer, "First-person: The Dying American Church," *SBC Baptist Press* (March 28, 2006), http://www.bpnews.net/bpcolumn.asp?ID=2197.

The problem is that most Christians and Christian ministries have only either an open or a closed hand. The result is *relevant heresy* among some liberals and *irrelevant orthodoxy* among some fundamentalists. Both groups fail to contend and contextualize equally; fundamentalists largely only contend, and liberals largely only contextualize. The Bible itself models this two-handed approach by giving us four Gospels. Each Gospel is written both to contend for the truth of the person and work of Jesus and to contextualize that truth to varying cultural groups so that the gospel is most easily understood by people in that culture. This explains why Matthew was written primarily to Jews by a Jew, Mark was written primarily to Romans, Luke was written primarily to Gentiles by a Gentile, and John was written to Greeks. They each tell the same truth, but with different emphases, language, and style, thus doing all they can to "win more of them . . . for the sake of the gospel," as Paul commands.

What I am not arguing for is *seeker-sensitive* Christianity where human felt-needs overshadow God's commands, and evangelism is reduced to marketing, which results in the rough edges of our faith being sanded off so that more customers shop at the church for religious goods and services. What I am arguing for is *seeker-sensible* Christianity.[76] Paul argues for seeker-sensible Christianity in 1 Corinthians 14; God's people were speaking a language that lost people simply could not understand, and Paul rightly commanded them to speak intelligible words in the church so that lost people could comprehend and be saved. Sadly, too often the church is filled with language, customs, and styles that are so altogether foreign to the average lost person that unless contextualization occurs and explanation is given, lost people will remain, in Paul's words, "foreigners" and not friends.

One of many examples Scripture gives us to illustrate all of this involves circumcision. On his various missionary journeys, Paul would take with him such people as Timothy and Titus. On those journeys, he had to decide how to deal with the very hotly debated cultural issue of circumcision, which distinguished the Jews from the Gentiles. More specifically, while both Timothy and Titus were uncircumcised, Paul had to determine whether or not to have both men circumcised in

---

[76]I want to thank my dear friend and fellow Acts 29 board member Ed Stetzer for his distinction on this point during his lecture at the Reform and Resurge conference (see http://theresurgence.com/r_r_2006_session_three_stetzer and http://theresurgence.com/r_r_2006_session_four_audio_stetzer).

light of the various cultural groups they would be ministering to. Paul decided to have Timothy circumcised,[77] but not Titus.[78] Why?

D. A. Carson was kind enough to send me a personal e-mail about this point. With his permission, I am including his insightful explanation. He said:

> Paul refuses to circumcise Titus, *even when it was demanded by many in the Jerusalem crowd*, not because it didn't matter to them, but because it mattered so much that if he acquiesced, he would have been giving the impression that faith in Jesus is not enough for salvation: one has to become a Jew first, before one can become a Christian. That would jeopardize the exclusive sufficiency of Jesus.
>
> To create a contemporary analogy: If I'm called to preach the gospel among a lot of people who are cultural teetotallers, I'll give up alcohol for the sake of the gospel. But if they start saying, "You cannot be a Christian and drink alcohol," I'll reply, "Pass the port" or "I'll think I'll have a glass of Beaujolais with my meal." Paul is flexible and therefore prepared to circumcise Timothy when the exclusive sufficiency of Christ is not at stake and when a little cultural accommodation will advance the gospel; he is rigidly inflexible and therefore refuses to circumcise Titus when people are saying that Gentiles must be circumcised and become Jews to accept the Jewish Messiah.

By giving two answers to the same question, was Paul being relative? No, he was being *relevant*. Was Paul being seeker sensitive? No, he was being *seeker sensible*. Why? Because he was doing all he could to "win more of them . . . for the sake of the gospel."

Admittedly, as the gospel passes from one culture to another there is the very difficult matter of determining what is to be *rejected*, what is to be *received*, and what is to be *redeemed*. This is true in both the culture that is sending and the culture that is receiving the gospel; the gospel will not be held captive to any culture without continually calling it, including church culture, to repentance. While Paul is specifically talking about prophecies, his general principle from 1 Thessalonians 5:21–22 is helpful: "Hold on to the good. Avoid every kind of evil" (NIV). This requires discernment, wisdom, the leading of the Holy Spirit, and a deeper understanding of a culture and its people than is possible from a distant glance.

---

[77] Acts 16:3
[78] Gal. 2:3

Learning to be relevant and seeker sensible is one of the reasons we have the New Testament epistles. Much of their content deals with the questions and conflicts regarding what was to be rejected, received, and redeemed as the gospel moved from the Jewish to the Gentile culture. Therefore, the New Testament is in itself a missiological example of the difficult theological work of contextualization. Today, this includes mode of dress, tattoos, piercings, plastic surgery, music styles, use of technology in church, entertainment (including television and film), smoking, drinking, and language. On many of these issues, many fundamentalist Christians are like their ancient pharisaical Jewish counterparts; they embrace numerous rules and assumptions on such cultural matters but lack clear theological and biblical support. Subsequently, Gentile postmoderns are now calling many of these cultural assumptions into question; they deserve the same kind of thoughtful, scriptural reflection that we see modeled in the New Testament epistles, and the same kind of humility from fundamentalists that newly converted Jews demonstrated when they willingly gave up their cultural elitism.

For example, in our day we must reject the rampant sexual sins of pornography, homosexuality, bisexuality, fornication, friends with benefits, and any and every other form of sexual deviancy because they are simply incompatible with Christian faith. Nevertheless, we cannot reject sex, because it was created by God and given to us as a very good gift. Therefore, we must do more than just tell our people to be virgins when they get married and to not commit adultery in marriage (though both are true). We must instead redeem sexuality as the Song of Songs does; sex is a gracious gift from God to be enjoyed only within heterosexual marriage. We must stress that while we reject sexual sin, we receive God's intention for sex and seek to redeem sex in our culture so that monogamous, pure, passionate heterosexual lovemaking is both free and frequent among God's people.

### The Cutting Edge?

In closing, some people will want to dismiss all of this as yet another faddish trend promoted by a young megachurch pastor devoted to giving an extreme makeover to the Puritans in order to promote cool

Calvinism. I will confess that in some ways this is all very cutting edge—the cutting edge of the sixteenth century.[79]

In the 1550s, John Calvin saw the population of his city of Geneva double as Christians fled there from persecution. Among the refugees was Englishman John Bale, who wrote: "Geneva seems to me to be the wonderful miracle of the whole world. For so many from all countries come here, as it were, to a sanctuary. Is it not wonderful that Spaniards, Italians, Scots, Englishmen, Frenchmen, Germans, disagreeing in manners, speech, and apparel, should live so lovingly and friendly, and dwell together like a . . . Christian congregation?"[80]

In his loving providence, God forced Geneva to become a short-term training ground in missions. Christians from varying cultures lived together there under the teaching of John Calvin, and they had to determine what to receive, reject, and redeem from their culture in order to effectively contextualize the gospel and do evangelism.

After they had such wonderful theological training and missiological experience, and after the persecution subsided, many of the Christians returned to their cultures. The result was an explosion of contending, contextualizing, and church planting. There were only five underground Protestant churches in France in 1555, but by 1562, 2,150 churches were planted, totaling some three million people. Furthermore, some of the churches were megachurches, with anywhere from four thousand to nine thousand people in attendance.

Additionally, church-planting missionaries were also sent by Calvin to Italy, the Netherlands, Hungary, Poland, and the free imperial city-states in Rhineland. The Atlantic Ocean was even crossed by church-planting missionaries, sent by Calvin to South America and present-day Brazil.

Because he was like Jesus and Paul in not merely his doctrine but also his practice, John Calvin rightly understood that God has both predestined the elect to be saved and predestined the church to be instruments of his election by contending and contextualizing in culture. He did this all for the sake of the gospel and was able to share in its blessings, including many people being saved and many churches being planted. I pray that is the fruit of the Reformed resurgence in our day as well.

---

[79]Lester De Koster, *Light for the City: Calvin's Preaching, Source of Life and Liberty* (Grand Rapids, MI: Eerdmans, 2004); Frank A. James III, "Calvin the Evangelist," *Reformed Quarterly* 19, no. 2/3 (Fall 2001), http://www.rts.edu/quarterly/fall01/james.html.
[80]Cited in James, "Calvin the Evangelist."

# Conversations with the Contributors

A t the conference from which this book is drawn, Justin Taylor led two conversations about issues related to the supremacy of Christ in a postmodern world. On September 29, 2006 he interviewed John Piper, Tim Keller, and Mark Driscoll.[1] The next day he interviewed John Piper, David Wells, D. A. Carson, and Voddie Baucham Jr.[2] What follows are lightly edited transcriptions of those conversations.

## John Piper, Tim Keller, and Mark Driscoll

JUSTIN TAYLOR:

Pastor John, in the summer of 2006 you spent two months poring over the commands of Jesus in the Gospels in order to write the book *What Jesus Demands from the World*.[3] I'm wondering what that amount of time spent with the words of Christ did for your own soul? Was there anything that you learned personally or took away from that time? Were you changed by doing that exercise?

JOHN PIPER:

First, it's a devastating thing to expose yourself to five hundred imperatives in the Gospels and dozens and dozens of demands from the One who has all authority in heaven and on earth, because his standards are so radical, going to the root of all your behaviors. Jesus is not concerned with what's on the outside, but he always is pressing down into the bottom: "Unless your righteousness exceeds that of the scribes and Pharisees" (Matt. 5:20)—their problem was they were whitewashed tombs.

So my preparation for the book was eleven weeks or so of

---

going deeper—having my heart exposed to its anger or impatience or unforgiveness—and clamoring then for the second impression, namely, that the Son of Man came into the world not to be served but to serve and to give his life a ransom for many (Mark 10:45). I didn't come to call the righteous but sinners (Luke 5:32). So you have this radical demand running side by side with these spectacular offers of mercy for those who will be the tax collector and despair of his own righteousness, instead of the Pharisee who is thanking God that he's worked in him righteousness and he's going to bank on it at the judgment day (Luke 18:9–14). So there was *hope*, and there was *desolation*—and if I understand the Gospels right, that's the way it's supposed to happen.

I think the personal effect of this preparation time was to intensify my desire to be in the face of a pluralistic world and to say as publicly and as provocatively as I can that all authority in the universe belongs to Jesus Christ. It doesn't belong to Muhammed, and it doesn't belong to any Hindu god. It doesn't belong to Moses. It belongs to Jesus Christ. And if you don't bow the knee to him, you will perish. We need to proclaim that God is angry at the whole world. If you don't obey the Son, the wrath of God rests on you. There's so much mealy-mouthed hesitancy to talk about the most important things in the world, namely, getting right with a holy God who will crush you forever if you don't go to the Son that he provided. I came away feeling like I just don't want to play games anymore. Life is short. I don't know how long I have. Jesus as he stands forth from the Gospels is spectacularly supreme and beautiful and glorious and tough and tender and worthy and attractive and satisfying. Why wouldn't you want to give your life to this?

JUSTIN TAYLOR:

All of us here believe in the supremacy of Christ. But there are different views among evangelicals concerning how Christ relates to culture. And Pastor Tim, this next question is for you. You've said the relationship of Christians to culture is the current crisis point for the church. Can you flesh out your understanding of the relationship between Christians and culture and the biblical way to influence culture?

TIM KELLER:

The classic book by Niebuhr, *Christ and Culture*,[4] lays out five approaches (and I've read so many interpretations of the book that I'm not totally sure what a couple of his approaches really represent). But there are five basic approaches: (1) withdraw from culture; (2) fit in with culture; (3) try to take over culture with a certain amount of political force; (4) just evangelize people (so if we change enough people's lives somehow the culture will change); and (5) the worldview-ish approach (you can't just convert people; you have to disciple them to think worldview-ishly). One person has said that there is probably both a healthy and an unhealthy version of each one of these five approaches to Christ and culture. So maybe there are ten approaches.

On one end of the spectrum is the *Christ against culture* approach, which creates a really thick countercultural Christian community. In Minneapolis, Bethlehem Baptist Church should not be just a group of evangelizing, discipling people, but an alternate, diverse city, showing Minneapolis what Minneapolis could look like under the lordship of Christ. And so, on the one hand, I'm real big on that idea of countercultural community—a really thick, different Christian society.

But then somehow, at the other end of the spectrum, there has to be *Christ transforming culture*—engagement to the rest of the city in service. You can't just go out there and serve without emphasizing the countercultural aspect, and you can't just emphasize the countercultural aspect without pressing the idea of service. What do I mean by service? Well, "service" can be defined as serving the needs of your community. Service is saying to the people around you, "We want to make this a good city for everybody to live in, and we're going to minister out of our difference. So we're going to give our income and care about the poor. We're going to be doing these things as a response to Jesus Christ, as he is in us and leading us. But it's going to benefit everybody. Everybody in the city is going to be benefited by us simply living out what Christ wants us to be."

The *Christ against culture* view is usually considered the Anabaptist approach; the other *Christ transforming culture* view is considered the Reformed approach. But I really think some kind of Reformed-Anabaptist approach is necessary—there's got to be some sort of merg-

4H. Richard Niebuhr, *Christ and Culture* (New York: Harper & Row, 1956).

ing of those two things, and it can't just be one pasted on top of the other. If you're countercultural without serving the rest of your city, it's selfish, and it's really not Christ. But on the other hand, if you're just out there serving people without creating these very thick, countercultural communities in which the values inside the community are very different from those outside the community, then in their passion for "justice," people will simply end up assimilating into the society.

JUSTIN TAYLOR:

So what if serving one group in the community is viewed as antagonistic to another? For example, if you want to serve unborn babies, wouldn't a lot of people view that as antagonistic too?

TIM KELLER:

In an article entitled "Soft Difference,"[5] Mirslav Volf points out from 1 Peter 2 that the pagans will glorify God through the good deeds of Christians—but it also assumes Christians will be persecuted too. And I think Volf is absolutely right in saying that if you live out the life Christ wants you to live, there will always be some overlap with your surrounding culture in which they will admire much of what you do, and they will be very offended by other things you do. So for example, if you're in the Middle East, Christian sex ethics are viewed as great. But the Christian approach to forgiveness would be considered stupid. In Manhattan, the Christian approach to forgiveness is wonderful, but the sex ethics are repressive. And so I think Volf is right in saying that wherever you are, if you simply live out your countercultural servant life, part of what you do will be attractive and part of what you do will be offensive, and you have to let the chips fall where they may. You will be a savior to those who are being saved, and you will be a stench to those who are not. So you will be both attractive and repulsive.

JUSTIN TAYLOR:

What about approaches to pop culture? Pastor Mark, you go to movies. You watch TV. You listen to modern music and go to comedy shows. Pastor John—you don't! So John, how do you stay *relevant*

---

[5]Mirslav Volf, "Soft Difference: Theological Reflections on the Relation Between Church and Culture in 1 Peter" (http://www.northpark.edu/sem/exauditu/papers/volf.html).

by mainly avoiding pop culture? And Mark, as you take part in pop culture, how do you stay *faithful* and *transformed* rather than being conformed?

MARK DRISCOLL:

I do believe, as Tim alluded to, that the two problems are *syncretism* and *sectarianism*. Syncretists go too far; sectarians don't go far enough. I think Jesus prayed against both in John 17:15: "I do not ask that you take them out of the world [that they would be removed from a lost, dying culture], but that you keep them from the evil one." And then he goes on in verse 17 to say, "Sanctify them in the truth; your word is truth." Jesus is praying for us, that we would be in this world with the people in this world but that we would be tethered to him through Scripture and truth, continually sanctified through Scripture so that we become neither accommodationists nor syncretists. Those who are culturally relevant without being biblically faithful tend to be *relevant heretics*, and those who are faithful to Scripture and removed from culture can sometimes be *irrelevant orthodox*; our goal should be *relevant orthodoxy*, to do like Paul says in 1 Corinthians 9: by all means to take as many opportunities to reach as many people as possible. And I think that is the continual tension of what it means to really be a missionary.

I would respectfully disagree with Niebuhr's approach to culture because the essence of *Christ and Culture* is mono-cultural, and we live now in a day of pluralism, diversity, and multi-culture. Not only are there five or ten views of culture; there are also hundreds of cultures and subcultures with their own values, languages, and tribes. As missionaries, how do we incarnate into culture to bring the truth of Jesus to a people group? Whether it's tattooed Indie rockers or hip-hoppers or orthodox Jews, whatever it might be—how do we do that faithfully? That's the missiological question. And that's where the tension between Christ and culture comes in. There's the left which says we should just be syncretists and not tethered to Scripture—and there are those who are more sectarian that say we should just stay tethered to Scripture, and buy canned goods, and hope for the rapture so that we could just leave (which is not very missional). The goal is to be like Jesus, who was fully in culture, fully identified with people, went to parties, had friends, participated in customs and such, never sinned, never did go too far, but went as far as he could to speak to people about the need for him and the repentance of sin that he demanded.

In Seattle, the city that I live in, I can't assume that the culture and the cultures that are there have any biblical mooring whatsoever. So to lose Scripture would be absolutely unfaithful to God, but to not have a way of communicating it effectively would really reduce the forward progress of the gospel, and I want both faithfulness and fruitfulness. That's always the tension.

JOHN PIPER:

My short answer is that I think I'm weak and therefore would probably become a carnal person if I plunged more deeply into movies than I do. That's the first answer: Piper's weak; he has to steer clear of certain kinds of things in order to maintain his level of intensity.

The second answer is that I think there are common denominators in human beings that are so massive that one can get a lot of mileage out of feeling them very strongly. For example, take the fact that *everybody's going to die*. You should try feeling that sometime. Just feel it. Everybody's going to die. And *everybody loves authenticity*. Try to feel that and go with that. People generally like to be held in suspense and then have something solved. I read the newspaper, listen to a little bit of NPR, and look at advertisers. I think they're the ones who study human beings, so I just try to read off what are they doing there. But mainly I'm trying to understand how John Piper ticks. I go deep with my own heart and my own struggles and my own fears and guilt and pride and then figure out how to work on that, and then from the Bible I tell others how they can work on that—and there's enough connection to be of some use.

JUSTIN TAYLOR:

Let me switch gears a little bit to the whole emerging-church conversation. John, you met recently with Tony Jones, who's the national coordinator for Emergent, and Doug Pagitt, who is also involved in the leadership of Emergent. Is there anything you can tell us about that meeting or anything that would be helpful to share about your time together with them? And how did it come about?

JOHN PIPER:

Tony and Doug took the initiative to e-mail me and asked if we'd be interested in meeting with them—I think because they read the blurb on this conference and were ticked off by it!

It was a very profitable time for me. I like these guys, by the way. I like them because I think they're both hotheads, and I think I am too. That was a personal impression. However, my root sense is that ultimately, for Tony and Doug, *committed relationships trump truth*. They probably would not like the word "trump" but would rather say that committed relationships *are* an authentic expression of the gospel, and that to ask, "What is the gospel underneath, supporting the relationships?" is a category mistake. And so I just kind of kept going back on my heels, saying I just don't understand the way these guys think. There are profound epistemological differences—ways of processing reality—that make the conversation almost impossible, as if we were just kind of going by each other. What is the function of knowledge in transformation? What are the goals of transformation? We seem to differ so much in our worldviews and our ways of knowing that I'm not sure how profitable the conversation was or if we could ever get anywhere.

Therefore I can't make definitive statements about what they believe about almost anything, except for a few strong statements about certain social agendas in which they would clearly come out of their chair on the hatred of human trafficking or something like that. But as far as their beliefs on certain doctrinal issues, I can't tell, because as I pushed on them, I could tell that their attitude was: "That's not what we do. That's not what we do here. We don't try to get agreement on the nature of the atonement. That is alienating to friendships to try to do that, so we don't do that." And because of that, I say, "Well, I don't even know where to start with you then." This shows how different we are, because Galatians 1:8 says, "If we or an angel from heaven should preach to you a gospel contrary to the one we preached to you, let him be accursed." And that's not friendship. Paul insists on establishing the gospel, whether there is a good relationship or not. I came away from our meeting frustrated and wishing it were different but not knowing how to make it different.

JUSTIN TAYLOR:

Mark, you're in the unique position of having been in both worlds—can you give us a recap of your journey, and how you went from being travel partners with Tony, Doug, and Brian McLaren to being at a Reformed gathering like this?

MARK DRISCOLL:

By the grace of a sovereign God, obviously. I'll tell you my story briefly. I was raised in an Irish Catholic working-class family. My dad worked to feed five kids by working as a union drywaller until he broke his back hanging drywall. My mom was charismatic Catholic, which I think means you pray in tongues to Mary (I'm not kidding). And so, as I grew up, I didn't know the Lord. In high school at the age of seventeen I met a beautiful gal, who was a pastor's daughter. She was the cutest gal I'd ever seen. She's here with me, my wife. And she said, "I'll only date a Christian." I said, "Well, praise the Lord!" And had she said, "I only date cowboys," I would have said, "Yee-hah!" So I started seeing her. And I kind of thought I was a Christian, because being a Catholic boy I thought that just meant you believed in God and were a good person. Well, I started reading the Bible that she gave me, and in college, at the age of nineteen, God saved me as soon as I started studying Augustine for philosophy and realized that sin is the problem. I didn't think I was a sinner until I read Augustine and learned that pride was a sin—then I realized I had all kinds of problems. And so God saved me in college. He spoke to me to start a church and to marry Grace and to plant churches and preach the Bible and do the things I'm doing now.

We got married and moved back to Seattle to start a church. I had not been to Bible college. I had not been to seminary. I'm in a city that is one of the least-churched cities in America. I started with a bunch of tattooed, pierced, chain-smoking, Indie rockers for a core group. Good luck taking ten guys committed to anarchy and making them into the foundation of an evangelical church! I started Mars Hill, and it was a really painful experience because I didn't know what I was doing. So I was looking for someone to talk to, to help me figure out what in the world I had gotten myself into.

I got a call from my friend Bob Buford of Leadership Network, and they were doing this young leader conference. So I ended up going to Mount Hermon, California, to speak at a pastors' conference. I'd never been to one. I didn't even know they had such things (I was kind of isolated up there in Seattle). There I spoke on the transition from the modern to postmodern world, and epistemological issues. This was almost a decade ago now. It opened a lot of national doors, and then we started traveling and doing conferences. Leadership Network put a speaking team together, and then they hired Doug Pagitt to oversee that group. As soon as they did, that's when I started having some friction. Personally, I hope that Doug would call me a friend, and we do know each other and have had a friendship in years past. But they were looking at things like open theism, female pastors, dropping the inerrancy of Scripture, penal substitutionary atonement, literal hell, those kinds of things. I was strongly evangelical and Reformed but moving toward even deeper Reformed convictions, and so that led to a real breech with where the group was going. Once Brian McLaren was brought on to travel and speak with us, that's when I hit the eject button, because I just knew that there was going to be a series of fights around the country, and I also knew that I was immature. Sometimes I would get angry and frustrated, curse, and act immaturely. Even in representing my side, I was not doing that well, so I decided to go home and work on my church and grow in my faith and repent of some sin in my own life—so that's what I did.

Since that time the Emergent movement has spun out of that, separate from Leadership Network. And then, in my church, God has blessed our Acts 29 network.[6] So I guess I broke off very, very, very early on; I was one of the early founders and then broke away from the movement. I find that there are more guys going that direction over some of these same theological issues, moving toward more of a Reformed and evangelical, historical, classic Protestant position.

JUSTIN TAYLOR:

Tim, if you could put on your prophet's hat for a minute, is the emerging church movement going to be a footnote in the history of evangelicalism, or is it going to be a chapter? Is it going to be more akin to the seeker movement, which clearly wasn't just a fading fad, but instead

---

[6]http://acts29network.org.

has lasted and is still lasting? Or will it simply be replaced in a few years with the next new thing?

TIM KELLER:

It depends. If you define evangelicalism in a kind of John Stott sort of way—that unlike liberals, evangelicals hold to historic Christian ortho- doxy, the authority of the Scripture, the deity of Christ, and so forth; but unlike fundamentalists, they are concerned about social justice and are more engaged in the culture—Stott would say that if you define evangelicalism that way, the seeker movement is inside evangelicalism. Its members would downplay and sort of put some of those cardinal doctrinal issues off to the side, but they don't deny them, whereas the Emergent church is moving away from that orthodoxy.

I do know that the liberal, mainline church has developed a kind of post-liberal reaction to the older liberalism—you can see it at places like Yale and Duke. It puts more emphasis on the canon. It puts more emphasis on reading the text. The commentaries that come out of this movement don't tear the book apart but actually try to listen for the text. They don't believe in inerrancy. They have a very different under- standing of truth. They would say that if the interpretive community says this is truth, then this is truth, and so on. Today's liberal mainline churches have moved away from the mainline older liberalism. It's less strident in some ways.

I think that in the same way, the emerging church represents a kind of post-conservativism. It's actually coming out in the very same spot. It's moving away from evangelical orthodoxy, and it has a lot in common with the post-liberals. In fact, the only difference between the post-conservatives and the post-liberals is what they used to be. The post-liberals used to be in mainline churches; the post-conservatives used to be in evangelical churches; and now they're coming together. I'm doubtful as to whether those two groups are going to become a cohesive movement, because I think they're going to have trouble. They don't have institutions, and I do think you need institutions. Evangelicalism developed in the United Kingdom and the United States because of certain institutions: a couple of key seminaries laid the groundwork for the movement, and Crusade, InterVarsity, and Navigators raised up the foot soldiers. Because of this, evangelicalism created something different. But I don't see that in the emerging church—it's so anti-institutional, so afraid of authority, that I doubt very much that it can create those institutions and become a cohesive movement. There might be some sort of post-liberal/post-conservative theological party that comes together, and I think it could produce writers and lots of books, but I doubt that they're going to create churches or any strong communities and institutions.

So I see Emergent churches moving away from what we would call "historic evangelicalism"—and no, I don't think it's going to be a strong movement. Though ten years from now I may be eating my words!

JUSTIN TAYLOR:

Mark, you've said the two hottest theologies today are Reformed theology and Emergent theology. On the Reformed track, why are tattooed, chain-smoking Indie rockers listening to John Piper and Tim Keller? Would you agree these are two of the most influential guys in your network?

MARK DRISCOLL:

Yeah, I think there are a few. Wayne Grudem's *Systematic Theology* has been very helpful.[7] C. J. Mahaney's influence has loosed up Reformed cessationism a little bit and opened the way for a lot of young guys who don't mind Reformed theology as long as it's not hardcore cessationist. They want to raise their hands and sing a little bit and not have anybody call them names. And I think the thing that makes Dr. Keller very appealing is his concept of urban missional engagement. There's a return among a lot of young people to the city, and there's a love for the city, and he's providing a theological-missiological framework that's very gospel-centric. Then there's Dr. Piper's commitment to the authority of Scripture, the supremacy of Jesus, and just flat-out passion. I think it's the passion that draws a lot of the young guys, because he seems to have encountered a Jesus that does more than just encourage him or motivate him. He's inspired by and passionate for the Jesus that he's met, and that makes people want to know that Jesus. I

---

[7]**Wayne Grudem,** *Systematic Theology: An Introduction to Biblical Doctrine* (Grand Rapids, MI: Zondervan, 1994).

think that those variables working together—the biblical passion, the urban missiology, and the non-cessationist freedom—are what I would consider the elements of the new Calvinism, I hope. I think they're good elements—freedom, mission, and Christ-exalting Bible theology—and a good, solid, rigorous place to begin.

JUSTIN TAYLOR:

John, I know that foreign missions are something that's almost always put on the back burner. With all this talk about North America itself being a mission field and all this talk about contextualization here, do you get concerned that foreign missions and going to people who have never heard the gospel in the first place are getting lost in all our talk about being missional and focusing on cities here in the United States?

JOHN PIPER:

I would be concerned about that if I saw good evidence of it. I don't know the Acts 29 movement well enough to know whether those churches that are planted feel that passion. I do get concerned about that, because I think the Great Commission is not anywhere near finished. I think the unreached peoples that are left to be reached are the hardest ones to reach. They tend to be Muslim or Hindu or Buddhist, and they tend to be poorer or very, very hostile. They don't want you to come, but that's no excuse for us not to go and proclaim Christ. And so, yes, it's a big concern.

I think there are two concerns. One is that, in the fascination with reaching Seattle, Christians there might simply be overworked and have no time to think about foreign missions. And why would you want to send away your best to India when there are so many to reach in Seattle? If I were talking with Mark about this issue, I would ask him about that and say, "How are you doing? Are you raising up an army to go to the unreached peoples?"

The second, more subtle concern I have is that I believe the seeker-sensitive way of doing contextualization is having a trickle-down effect in missiological contextualization in a very harmful way. And I think it is partly influenced by fear—fear of not succeeding—so that if you go to an Islamic people, and they will not use the term

"Son of God" and want to be called Muslim, then you just adjust. You say, "Okay, we won't call Jesus 'Son of God,' and we'll call you a Muslim follower of Jesus." And if they want to read the Koran, you say, "Okay, you read the Koran. That's a good, holy book, but be sure you read the Bible also." That sounds so chic and American. And so foreign missions can be undermined both ways: (1) just forget that they're there, or (2) go with a compromised message or a view of contextualization that is driven by fear, because you could get yourself poisoned.

As I read the New Testament and the radical Jesus that we serve, what's so mind-boggling to me is that some of the main Emergent leaders talk about how Jesus has been domesticated by the church, and they want to recover the "radical Jesus." In my judgment, the Jesus they're recovering is not radical. There is no radical Jesus without hell. Everything becomes Milquetoast without the wrath of God. He came into the world to rescue us from the most horrid thing in the world. And once you get that straight, then having your head chopped off is minor. It's minor because we don't fear those who can kill the body and after that have nothing more that they can do. Who talks like that today in America? "Do not fear those who kill the body but cannot kill the soul. Rather fear him who can destroy both soul and body in hell" (Matt. 10:28). If you strip that away from Jesus, he's a local guy. He's just no big deal.

"Through many tribulations we must enter the kingdom" (Acts 14:22)—that's the message that I think will make an army of missionaries go finish this thing. And it *will* be finished. Jesus said so: "This gospel of the kingdom will be proclaimed throughout the whole world as a testimony to all nations, and then the end will come" (Matt. 24:14).

JUSTIN TAYLOR:

Tim, switching gears back to the domestic front. How do you counsel professionals in Manhattan to think about their vocation? It seems to me that there are the two extremes. There's the secret Christian that nobody at work even knows is a believer, and the other guy who's always leaving tracts in the bathroom stall. Where's the middle ground? How can people be appropriately missional at work?

TIM KELLER:

Generally speaking, I believe that what you want is Christians to think out ways of applying the gospel that are *counterintuitive* but at the same time *attractive* to other members of their vocational field. They need to let the gospel shape the way in which they work.

You know, a great example of this is a Christian guy named Mike who came to Redeemer. He got a vision for integrating his faith with his work—he saw an area of the financial world in which he knew that certain companies making major real-estate prices had to rely on a kind of company that gave them information. Mike discovered that most of the people in this field were gouging their customers, because if their customers were more well-informed, they could make better choices. He said, "I could bring some justice and some fairness into a field and still make a ton of money, because if I go out there, and I'm just more honest and open with my customers—explaining that I'm here to serve you instead of use you—everybody is going to come to me." And that's exactly what happened. Within a couple of years, he really made a certain part of the field more transparent. Buyers and sellers know better what's going on, but he's still making a ton of money. His company's grown enormously. And he's spun off five or six nonprofits to do work in the community. Mike constantly says to everybody, "You don't have to be a Christian to work in this company, but it is based on Christian principles. You don't have to be a Christian, but you need to know that we do what we do because of service, honesty, and integrity." His Christian faith has had a great deal of impact, not only in his company, but also in his field. It's not just, *Oh, I'm doing well in my field and so people are going to listen to my testimony*. He has to deal with integrity. There's got to be some kind of overlap between what he does and his beliefs, and then he's got an opportunity to speak in a much more organic way about his faith.

Proclaiming Christ in the workplace is complicated. Part of the real problem is that we pastors don't know the vocational world, and the people in the vocational world don't know theology. It's very, very difficult for people to build those kinds of bridges. For example, the first time I experienced this was when a young man who was a soap-opera actor became a Christian at Redeemer. He was on the soaps in New York, and he sat down with me right away and started asking me questions. He said, "I've become a Christian, and I want to know what you think of method acting?" I said, "What's method acting?" He says, "Well, in method acting, you don't act angry; you get angry." I said, "Well, that doesn't sound very good. For example, what about lust?" "Yeah," he says. "Okay. That's really not very good," I said. He started asking me all kinds of questions, and I realized I knew nothing about the acting field. He clearly saw there were all sorts of implications of Christianity that had to do with his field. I didn't know the field; he didn't know theology. We had to spend a great deal of time. He had to educate me, and I had to educate him.

We ministers don't like that. We went to seminary! We know all about it. But if you're going to actually help people integrate faith with their work, they have to educate you as much as you have to educate them. You're working on it together, and that is very, very different from the way in which I do other kinds of discipling and training. It's really a very complicated field of discipleship.

### David Wells, D. A. Carson, Voddie Baucham, and John Piper

JUSTIN TAYLOR:

Dr. Wells, I want to start with you. Many people today are identifying themselves as "spiritual" but not "religious." What's the significance of this, and do you see it as an encouraging sign?

DAVID WELLS:

I do actually think this is an extraordinary moment, culturally speaking. Some of us are old enough to remember the literature of the seventies, and we remember those days when the advocates of secular humanism thought they were about to be triumphant, and the opponents of it feared the same thing, and so we debated back and forth.

But what has happened in the last couple of decades is really quite extraordinary. While it is true that secular-humanistic attitudes are located in some cultural pockets—we have them in academia, in Hollywood, and everywhere in Massachusetts—in the wider public, apparently almost 80 percent of people are increasingly defining themselves and thinking of themselves as being spiritual people. Peter Berger has this rather apt illustration. He says America is like the nation of

Indians ruled by Swedes. In other words, the cultured elites are trying to preside over a people who are very spiritual. And so there are these constant conflicts. But, like anything, when you have a cultural shift, there are pluses and minuses. There are things that become easier and things that become more difficult.

When the Enlightenment and secular humanism seemed to be so triumphant, the Christian gospel, which was about spirituality through Christ, seemed so out of step. Now the gospel about spirituality through Christ is just one among many, because everybody's into spirituality from all kinds of sources. The lines of division have shifted and changed. The frontier of the gospel is now a little bit different. And in particular, I think it's what we have been talking about here of the exclusive access to what is redemptively spiritual through Christ. That's the point at which people get frustrated with us.

JUSTIN TAYLOR:

Dr. Carson, I want to turn to you next. One of the things so many of us appreciate about you is that you not only write learned commentaries on biblical books and social issues, but you actually go out to the universities and do missions. I wonder if you could tell us what has changed in the last three decades among the students that you interact with, and how your message has changed in response to the changing attitudes of the students.

D. A. CARSON:

Well, I sometimes say that thirty or thirty-five years ago in a university mission, if I were dealing with an atheist, at least he or she was a Christian atheist—that is, the God in which he or she did not believe was more or less the Christian God. You can't even assume that anymore. Today, the biggest thing to come to terms with is the massive biblical ignorance. There just is very little residual knowledge, or even cultural heritage, of the Bible. You deal with people nowadays who don't know the Bible as two testaments. They've certainly never heard of Abraham or Isaiah, and if they've heard of Moses, they confuse him with Charlton Heston or a recent cartoon figure, depending on how up-to-date they are.

Because of this, full-orbed gospel preaching means starting farther back. Now there are lots of spin-offs on that regarding how you do missions. It used to be that participants in a university mission week would follow up with the people who got converted during the week. To be honest, I rarely see people converted in university missions today during the few days that I'm there. But it becomes the setup for ongoing Bible studies and explorer groups, and the fruit comes in during the following three months. It's just the way it is. There is more diversity and more backgrounds that students come from. On the other hand, there was a period when big university missions were just about gone. Nobody was doing them, but now they are starting to come back again.

In one sense, a lot of the new generation is so biblically illiterate, they're less antagonistic. Twenty-five years ago, enough of them had some sort of vague Christian background that they were quite sure what they were against. This new generation is so ignorant that, provided they're approached with a certain amount of respect, they don't have an automatic negative reaction quite so much (not nearly as much as their parents did, in my view). So again, there's an openness and an alien status to the whole thing. University missions today are for me a lot more fun than they were twenty-five years ago. They were more confrontational twenty-five years ago than they are now.

JUSTIN TAYLOR:

What do you have to do differently as a result of that changing situation?

D. A. CARSON:

It depends how many meetings I have. Sometimes when you go somewhere, you only have two or three meetings, so you can't do a whole series then. But if I have a chance at a whole series—five, seven, eight, or more over a few days—then I usually start with creation. The first message is called "The God Who Makes Everything." I expound Genesis 1–2—who God is, what creation means, its significance, the foundations of everything, the beginning of right and wrong, the grounding of our responsibility before God—and try and play that out in terms of how we look at everything. The second message is "The God Who Does Not Wipe Out Rebels," from Genesis 3—the nature of sin and rebellion, the curse, and where death comes from—to set things up. And then, depending on how many slots they give me, "The God Who Legislates" is the next message, where I cover the Ten Commandments and a chunk of Leviticus. And eventually I get to "The God Who Becomes a Human Being" where I deal with John 1:1–18; and then Romans 3:21–26, "The God Who Declares the Guilty Just," in the context of the first three chapters of Romans. If I have enough sessions, the last two are "The God Who Is Very Angry" and "The God Who Triumphs," based on Revelation 21–22.[8] So it's trying to create the whole biblical narrative while at the same time dropping in all the crucial systemic structures that make Christianity cohere and apply it to life.

One of the problems, however, is that it's very rare today to get a university mission that gives me all the sessions I want. So that's one of the changes. Everything is in two days and three days nowadays. And so I'm having to adapt again. It's just very difficult to paint a holistic picture in two hours.

JUSTIN TAYLOR:

One of the things that Tim Keller said in his presentation was that he doesn't know of a short gospel presentation that weds biblical theology and systematic theology and tells the storyline of the Bible. Do you agree with that? Is there anything out there that you would recommend?

D. A. CARSON:

There are better things and worse things. I take Tim's point that there isn't anything that gets that marriage really, really, really well. But there are a lot of books and small guides out there that are not bad to use. Vaughn Roberts in Oxford has produced a book, *God's Big Picture*,[9] that I sometimes give away. I've adapted *The Two Ways to Live*[10] somewhat for my own usage. There are resources like that around because, when you're training others to do evangelism and they're brand-new baby Christians, you have to give them something. You

---

[8]Dr. Carson's evangelistic messages are available for purchase at http://christwaymedia.com.
[9]Vaughan Roberts, *God's Big Picture* (Downers Grove, IL: InterVarsity Press, 2003).
[10]Tony Payne and Philip Jenson, *The Two Ways to Live* (Kingsford, Australia: Matthias Media, 2003). See also http://twowaystolive.com.

can't say, "Wait until you have at least three degrees in biblical theology and two more in systematic theology before you can start." You have to start from somewhere.

On the other hand, Tim is surely right to say that we need some more serious thought in this area of how to wed biblical and systematic theology together in telling, succinct ways.

Justin Taylor:

Dr. Baucham, you go to a lot of universities as well, and I've heard that you've developed an approach called "expository apologetics." Is that the same thing that we're talking about here, or is it something different?

Voddie Baucham:

It is a little different. I would define it as a commitment to biblical exposition that has developed out of my ministry over the years. I deal with a lot of question-and-answer sessions and things of that nature, and I finally came to the conclusion that basically, there are no new objections to the gospel. The gospel message hasn't changed, and so the essence of the objections hasn't changed—although they may be worded differently or come from different perspectives. The Bible writers, particularly in the New Testament, were actually dealing with and answering these very objections. And if we will learn those basic categories of objections and learn biblical passages in context that deal with those categories of objections, we can give answers that, first of all, are *memorable* because they come from a biblical text in context. Secondly, they're *authoritative* because they come from biblical texts in context. And thirdly, they give us "hooks" to hang our thoughts on.

I'll give you an example. One of the categories people are always asking about is revelation: the development of the canon, how the Bible came to be, and all these sorts of things. And so I developed an answer based on 2 Peter 1:16–21. People ask me, "Why do you believe the Bible?" And I say, "Because it's a reliable collection of historical documents written down by eyewitnesses during the lifetime of other eyewitnesses. They report supernatural events that took place and fulfilled the specific prophecies, and they claim that their writings are divine rather than human in origin." That answer is just an exposition of 2 Peter 1:16–21, where Peter was dealing with that very issue. And so what I try to do is use those texts in context to answer the objections that are raised in these various categories, so that the answers are thoroughly biblical, memorable, authoritative, and impactful.

JUSTIN TAYLOR:

Dr. Wells, in reading *Above All Earthly Pow'rs* I was struck by a footnote where you listed a number of articles that you've written over the years.[11] Your self-description there is that you were writing on "the missional nature of theology." So, long before Mark Driscoll was probably born, you were the "missional theologian"! Can you explain what you mean by contextualization and being missional? How can people as different as you and Mark Driscoll both be missional and be concerned with the contextualization of the gospel?

DAVID WELLS:

Actually it was really funny, as I was listening to Mark, because he sounded so far out, so testing the boundaries, pushing the envelope. Now when *I* say those very same things, I sound staid and tame. It's not right—I want to be hip, man!

In *Above All Earthly Pow'rs* I recount a scene in a novel that I found very telling.[12] It concerns an imaginary country called Sarkhan. The country's ambassador was an American who has lost his seat in Congress and wanted a judgeship. That didn't work out, so he settled for being an ambassador to Sarkhan. He did not believe in trying to understand the history and the customs of the people of Sarkhan, and he discouraged the embassy staff from doing that too. And in this account, the United States sends off to Sarkhan a gift of rice, and so it's carried to Sarkhan in American ships, transported in American trucks. It is a wonderful ceremony. There are all these American officials standing around, making a formal presentation of this gift. What they don't realize is that some Communists sneaked in and stenciled "This Is a Gift from Russia" on the bags of rice, written in Sarkhanese. So here you have the American officials making these very formal speeches

---

[11]David Wells, *Above All Earthly Pow'rs* (Grand Rapids, MI: Eerdmans, 2005), 9 n. 5. The referenced note is reproduced in chapter 1 n. 3 of this present volume.
[12]Ibid., 10–11. The novel referenced is *The Ugly American* by William Lederer and Eugene Burdick.

about this gift that they're giving, and the problem was they didn't understand the language. They didn't know what was actually happening and what the people understood from the ceremony.

And it struck me that this was just one more illustration of some of the things that have been mentioned here by Tim and by Mark. Theology is undoubtedly about timeless truth that we have in Scripture under the inspiration of the Holy Spirit. But it is timeless truth that needs to be brought by God's people into their own particular context. This, right now, has become a very agitated discussion right across the front, and it's especially interesting in missionary circles. There is a movement now among some missiologists who are arguing not simply that missionaries should adapt the culture of the place where they go—dressing like them, learning their customs, language, history (what the ambassador should have done in Sarkhan)—but they've actually gone one step further and argued that people can receive Christ within the context of other religious cultures such as Hinduism and Islam. They can receive Christ without leaving those contexts and religions. So in this missionary context you really don't have a church, because, of course, a church would very often imperil Christians: the moment they're baptized, they get killed. This is a way, they're arguing, to penetrate these cultures.

Here, in my judgment, a line has been crossed that is fatal to the gospel and to Christian faith, and derogatory to Christ. What you really have is a synthesis, the paganism of the Old Testament against which the prophets prophesied. We can't have Christ and these other religions, but we also can't have Christ and our own cultural practices where those practices and those beliefs violate what an understanding of Christ and a following of Christ requires. So it requires discernment on our part to see how we can get alongside people and speak their language, learning what habits, practices, and customs we can adopt without violating the truth, but also how that timeless truth can be made to intersect with the way in which people think.

I happen to believe principally in expository preaching. But if I have a critique of expository preachers, it is that some of them think that once they have unpacked the truth of a text, they've done their work. And sometimes this is reinforced by the belief that the Holy Spirit will accomplish what they haven't done. God in his grace undoubtedly does do that, but if simply reading the Bible was sufficient, why would God have given to the church teachers and preachers or teaching preachers? Preachers need to take that additional step. And especially here in America—as people are coming out of an increasingly paganized culture where the Christian memory gets more and more distant, where people in the pews understand less and less or bring less and less of a Christian worldview with them—it becomes more and more imperative for preachers to make sure that the truth they are preaching intersects with what is going on inside people's minds. The line must be drawn so clearly that people in their own lives know whether they are being obedient or not, and what they should do with that truth when they have heard it. Now *that* is contextualization. It goes all the way from people sitting in pews in America to missionaries who are doing their evangelism in a Hindu or Islamic context.

JUSTIN TAYLOR:

Dr. Carson, do you have any books that you would recommend or pastor models that you would commend that "do" evangelistic preaching in the church context particularly well?

D. A. CARSON:

I strongly recommend that you buy tapes or download messages from preachers who have a reputation for handling the Word well and for seeing genuine conversions by the declaration of the whole counsel of God. And don't listen to just one. Listen to half a dozen. If you'll only listen to one, the tendency is that you will try and mimic that person, and it might not really be you. Listen to eight or ten strong preachers who are really quite different, and the irony is that you then have freedom to be more of yourself while still learning to pick up the best from other folk. So by all means listen to John Piper.[13] Listen to Tim Keller.[14] Listen to Mark Driscoll.[15] And see how they go after the fundamentals of faith by handling texts—Scripture after Scripture after Scripture—again and again and again and again.

There are other things that you can do. It depends a bit on the

---

[13]http://desiringgod.org
[14]http://sermons.redeemer.com
[15]http://media.marshillchurch.org

country and the culture you are in. Fifty years ago, a lot of people in the Western world—both in Britain and in North America, and elsewhere—would designate Sunday morning for worship and Sunday evening for evangelistic services. That's gone—completely gone. But on the other hand, I know quite a few churches in the English-speaking world (though not many in North America) that will have "guest services." That doesn't mean they don't want guests to come to church any other time, but they hold special services where the whole congregation is encouraged in advance to pray for particular friends and neighbors and people they've been talking to about the Lord, and then invite them to those guest services. Now the wrong way to do a guest service is then to make it so cutesy, so relevant in all the wrong senses, so dumbed down, that it's a sham, and the whole thing feels inauthentic. Instead, all you do in a guest service is work extra hard at explaining everything. All that's doing is cutting down the pressure and the tension.

For example, before the first song is sung, something like this could be said: "Christians have a lot to sing about. In this church we join Christians from across the century in singing things that were sung sixteen hundred years ago, four hundred years ago, one hundred years ago, and ten weeks ago. Our first song was written by an ex-slave trader by the name of John Newton. When the music starts, you will find the words in the overhead screen, and we'll stand to sing them together."

Prayer can be introduced like this: "God is a talking God, and he likes to hear us talk to him. When we talk to him, we call it prayer. That's all we mean by it. In our church we find it helpful to shut our eyes and bow our heads in reverent adoration and to shut out other things. This may seem strange to you. That's all right. But you listen as we address our most holy, reverent, and wonderful God. Let us pray." Then the whole congregation bows in prayer. And you don't pray for three minutes of cutesy stuff: "Oh, heavenly Father we just want to thank you for being here!" You make your prayer full of gravitas and joy and the wonder of God and so on, and people will go out even if they haven't understood it all, saying, "Truly God has met us in this place."

In guest services, go for authenticity but make it a little more user-friendly. You can do that in any church, can't you, if you start building up a culture of friendliness toward outsiders? In large part, a good church is doing something of that almost all the time. People are getting converted under the ordinary ministry of the Word.

JUSTIN TAYLOR:

I imagine that a lot of pastors could be discouraged with the size of their church. They may have a smaller church, and then they see Mark Driscoll talking. He preaches substitutionary atonement, and eight hundred people come to church the next week. *They* preach substitutionary atonement, and eight people leave the next week. What sort of encouragement would you give to the small-town or rural pastor who feels that, in order to benefit from this conference, he has to drop everything and move to the city to make a difference for Christ?

JOHN PIPER:

I would say that feeding the flock of God is the most precious and high and glorious calling in the world. Jesus said to Peter three times in John 21, "Feed my sheep. Feed my sheep. Feed my sheep—and don't ever give up." There's always room for growth. We can always do better. I come away from conferences like these discouraged. Don't you? Every one of these guys discourages me. I just keep thinking: I'm not doing *that* well; I'm not doing *that* well; I'm not doing *that* well. . . . But that's life. It's a great thing to rest in the calling that God has given you and to cherish the Word of God. To study it and to explain it and to apply it and to exalt over it is the highest calling I know.

Now, there has to be witness in rural areas. (As Tim Keller would be the first to say.) I mean, it would just be absurd to say that we shouldn't have churches in small towns or in the country. Tim wouldn't say that. He's outraged at the abandonment of the cities. Something's askew when evangelicals leave the city. It's not that everybody should go to the city, but what has caused such an exodus? What's going on there that needs to be redressed? And there are enough people right here to fix both of those problems. We can have churches in the small towns and churches in the city. So God calls people in different ways, and he gifts people in different ways, and there are pastors who flourish in small towns.

Now you have to have different expectations in a small town because if there are eight hundred people in the town—and there's a charismatic church, a Roman Catholic church, a Lutheran church, and you're the pastor of a Baptist church—everybody's aligned already. The lines are drawn. Everybody knows where everybody stands. There are, say, ten families who don't go to church, and everybody knows who they are. Now what is a mission like that supposed to look like? Faithful, loving exposition, feeding, growing up, reaching out, forming relationships—it's got to look different. You can't be beat up by an urban pastor who says you have to go out and dress like the people you're trying to reach. You might say, "Everybody dresses the same in this town." Absolutely. Everybody's the same. And so be encouraged that God loves rural people, and God loves his church in rural situations, and God loves his Word, and God loves the faithful exposition of his Word, and God loves the faithful pastor showing up at a funeral or at a sick bedside. God loves all those things. Every place has its own different challenges, and a small town is a glorious place. Sometimes I think I'd just like to go there and pastor a flock without all the complications of suburbs and campuses and multiple worship services and complicated staffing where you're trying to draw charts that make sense and have small groups all over the place. And wouldn't that be nice if the church was just a small group and you knew everybody by name? That's a glorious calling.

D. A. CARSON:

There are different degrees of gifting. If we're doing something wrong that we can fix within the gift and calling God has given us, and a conference like this helps us fix it, even if it is just one or two small things, then—in addition to the encouragement from the Word—that's a good thing.

I was brought up in French Canada. As recently as 1972, in a population of 6.5 million, there were thirty-five or thirty-six evangelical churches, none with more than forty people. Between 1972 and 1980 the churches grew from about thirty-five to just under five hundred, many of them with hundreds of members. But in 1972, my father was a church planter through all those lean years when Baptist ministers alone spent eight years in jail for preaching the gospel. The charges were always "inciting to riot" or "disturbing the peace," but that's what it was. We kids would get beaten up in the 1950s because we were *maudite protestant*—damn Protestants. In all those years my father saw virtually no fruit. I remember many times seeing him in tears for his people. In 1972, when the turn came, he was already sixty-one years old, and the leadership passed off into other hands. In that period of growth I know he felt as if he had been largely put on the shelf. But when he died at the age of eighty-one—although he still felt that way—in fact, most of the church in Quebec viewed him as the grand old man because he had been faithful through the lean years.[16]

There are people who went to Korea in 1900, planted churches, and saw the church grow to a quarter of the world's evangelical population today. There are people who went to Japan about the same time—and no place on God's green earth did the church grow more slowly than in Japan. What are you going to do? Say, "All the ones who went to Korea are spiritual—particularly loved of God?" The ones in Japan aren't blessed of God? God works on another scale.

I made a resolution when I was a young man that I would never, so help me God, for the rest of my life, ever accept or reject any speaking invitation whatsoever on the basis of either size or honorarium. I kept that promise. Otherwise you only will end up going to bigger and bigger and bigger things. There's something dishonorable about that when Christ comes for the poor and the needy and starts with twelve, but one turns out to be a traitor, another denies him, and the rest run away. Don't let this crowd fool you. Learn the best things from it, and rejoice in the encouragement. Rejoice with those who rejoice and, if you are less gifted, be faithful where you are and be thankful.

JUSTIN TAYLOR:

Dr. Baucham, I want to ask you about the issue of race that you brought up earlier when you said that blacks and whites in the church. . . .

VODDIE BAUCHAM:

"Blacks—and the not-so black."

[16]The story is told more fully in D. A. Carson, ed., *Memoirs of an Ordinary Pastor: The Life and Reflections of Tom Carson* (Wheaton, IL: Crossway Books, forthcoming).

JUSTIN TAYLOR:

That's right! Rebuke accepted. There are a lot of white churches that could frankly care less about having diversity within them. But there are also a number of evangelical churches that long for greater diversity and don't see it happening. They don't know how to bring that about. What are your thoughts on that? And how would you counsel us—mainly a white audience—to increase the diversity within the church as the body of Christ?

VODDIE BAUCHAM:

I don't think you even knew this when you decided to ask me that question, but the church that we just planted in April right now has about 150 people in it, and because of the church's location, my family is the only black family in the church. I have had a very interesting journey in ministry because I have served in predominantly black churches—that's another thing that I think is very ironic. People always look at churches that are predominantly white and say, "Oh, where's the diversity?" There are very few predominantly black churches that have any diversity, and nobody's saying, "Oh, why are they all black?" I took a staff position in a predominantly white church just because of a passion that I had for people who are not like me. It was a turbulent time for my family and for me, and I write about it in *The Ever-Loving Truth*.[17] It was as though we were homeless. We were rejected by black people because now we were sellouts. Ironically, on the one hand, black people were talking about doors that weren't open—I walked through an open door, so now I'm a sellout. And on the other hand, there we were in a context where, for the lack of a better term, our "soul language" was not spoken. The language of our soul was not spoken in this other cultural context. But it was as though God had called us to be missionaries to the not-so-black people. And we've been doing that for a while now. I'm excited that we have some Asian and Hispanic families who come.

But that's where I live. I live in one of the most ethnically diverse cities in America. There are over sixty-five foreign consulates and 120 language groups in Houston—it's one of the most ethnically diverse

---

[17]Voddie Baucham Jr., *The Ever-Loving Truth: Can Faith Thrive in a Post-Christian Culture?* (Nashville: B&H, 2001).

cities that there are. And so for us, the expectation of diversity is more reasonable than for people who live in a less diverse place.

I've actually sat down with pastors who were burdened over the issue of diversity and said to them, "I haven't been here long, but as we ride around I'm wondering, 'Where are these people who are not like you going to come from?'" And they've never thought about that before! Dr. Carson writes about this in *The Gagging of God*[18]—the idea of empirical pluralism, church pluralism, and philosophical pluralism. Somewhere along the line, the idea of church pluralism has crept in—the idea that something that is more *diverse* is by definition *better*. I think that's a dangerous idea. Just because something is more diverse doesn't necessarily mean that it's better. There are some places where churches are very diverse just because they are in an area where that's the reality. They haven't tried to do that. They don't have a passion for that. And there are other places where people are passionate for biblical reasons about this diversity that God gives us, but for whatever reason they are not in an environment where they can see that come to fruition. Are they worse off? To go back to Dr. Carson's example of Japan versus Korea—are these people worse off just because they don't see as many different shades of people in their congregations?

Instead of asking how much diversity we have or how little diversity we have, we need to deal with the issue of the sin of racism and the sin of classism. If we are not diverse because we are sinful, and we do not love people who are not like us, we need to get on our faces before God rather than looking at it just as something that we can check off in our book, so to speak.

D. A. CARSON:

As a seminary professor, I look at things from the point of view of analyzing my students. And every year I keep an eye on the *M.Div-ers* who can speak to anybody. We have some guys at Trinity who are going to be great pastors in Lincoln, Nebraska. God bless them. That's where they're from. That's what they're like. That's what they're called to. May their tribe multiply.

In my formation group a year or so ago we had an African-American dude from the slums of Detroit. Anything bad that could

---

[18]D. A. Carson, *The Gagging of God* (Grand Rapids, MI: Zondervan, 2002).

have happened to him, happened to him—and he caused most of it too! But he's been wonderfully saved. And he's going to be great in districts amongst his own people—he is. But let's face it. He's not going to make it in Minneapolis.

On the other hand, there are some—no matter what color they are, what background they're from, or how much education they've had—who seem to be gifted by God with the ability to talk to anybody. And those are the people that I want in our cities. I want them to be pastored by people who are themselves able to talk to anybody. As demographics change in this country, they are going to be some of the pastors of the future. So without discounting anything that Voddie said, I also think that there are more and more cities on the coasts, increasingly in the center of the country, and lastly in the South, where there will be more and more cities with racially mixed churches, racially mixed areas, racially mixed districts, and so on where, to be quite frank, color isn't all that important. We need pastors who are leading that, spearheading it and understanding it. I keep telling my students there are some ways in which Los Angeles is more like heaven than Fargo, North Dakota, because in heaven there will be people from every tongue and tribe and people and nation. We want pastors like that for those cities.

JUSTIN TAYLOR:

Dr. Wells, this will be the final question. You've written so winsomely and compellingly in your four-volume series[19] on the dangers of consumerism, the need to cultivate authenticity in this postmodern climate, the need to exalt the supremacy of Christ, and the need to cling to the cross. Can you tell us what you do in your own personal life to cultivate humility and to draw closer to the Savior so that you're not drawn into the temptations of consumerism and the tyranny of the urgent?

DAVID WELLS:

Well, I hardly think I'm a paragon of virtue in these things. You know, they're easier to write about than to practice. I will tell you that I have been just extremely grateful for the opportunity that's come my way

---

[19]*No Place for Truth: or, Whatever Happened to Evangelical Theology?* (1994); *God in the Wasteland: The Reality of Truth in a World of Fading Dreams* (1995); *Losing Our Virtue: Why the Church Must Recover Its Moral Vision* (1999); *Above All Earthly Pow'rs: Christ in a Postmodern World* (2006). All published by Eerdmans.

to go to Africa every year. I do so in connection with Rafiki,[20] which builds orphanages mostly for kids left behind by AIDS. Every year when I go, I do a pastors' conference in the city where we are and have an opportunity (brief as it is) to sit down and talk with some of these pastors. After every encounter I realize how easy the circumstances under which I live become normal. This is normal life. The reality is that it is America that is highly abnormal when you look around the world. If you look at the big picture, it's just highly abnormal for people to have so many choices, to have supermarkets like we have, and everything else that goes with our consumerism. It's not that the things in themselves are evil, but it is the way in which we come to think about our lives as really consisting in all of our options and things that we can buy, which we sometimes use to create identities and prestige for ourselves.

Every time I go to Africa, I'm just brought up sharp on this point. This last time I did a conference somewhere in Malawi, and what struck me there was that out of all the pastors I talked to, there wasn't one of them who only had one church. Actually the smallest number was four, and one had fourteen. Fourteen churches! Do you know what it's like? Can you imagine what it's like to be a pastor with fourteen churches to look after? And remember who's in these churches—you've got people who are dying of AIDS all the time. In Africa, the nuclear family is a thing of the past, because any adults who are left standing have responsibility for the kids that remain. In a family you'll have, perhaps, the children of the husband and wife, and then you've got the kids of the brother and the aunt and the sister and all the way down. Households can reach up to ten, twelve, or fourteen kids, and then they can't take anymore. So these are the people who are in the church.

I talk to these pastors and I realize I'm just living in a different universe. I'm dealing with life that is so different from what they are looking at day after day. I plan my retirement, but in Africa, life expectancy now in most countries is the upper thirties. They have no retirement.

So you begin to see these things, and I have found that for me—and I am answering this rather personally—this has been, I think, one of the greatest, most salutary experiences. I come back from this and think that all of the things that have seemed to be so important,

---

[20]http://www.rafiki-foundation.org/

that so preoccupied me and defined how life is and what's a normal life, it's just not so. These are surface things. And I really need to try to focus on the really important things that lie underneath.

JOHN PIPER:

Let's pray.

*Father, I pray earnestly that as we hold in our left hand the most precious treasures in the world you would give the extraordinary wisdom that we need to do the right hand well. We want to reach lost people, and we don't want to give away the gospel in the process. Who is sufficient for these things? May we all, O God, believe truth and live it out more effectively, more winsomely, more compellingly than we ever have. I pray in Jesus' name. Amen.*

# Subject Index

# Scripture Index

# ⚜ desiringGod

If you would like to ponder further the vision of God and life presented in this book, we at Desiring God would love to serve you. We have produced hundreds of resources to help you grow in your passion for God and help you spread that passion to others.

At our website, desiringGod.org, you'll find almost all of the resources John Piper has written and preached, including more than 30 books. We've made over 25 years of his sermons available free for you to read, listen to, download, and in some cases watch online. In addition, you can access hundreds of articles, listen to our daily internet radio program, find out where John Piper is speaking, learn about our conferences, discover our God-centered children's curricula, and browse our online store.

John Piper receives no royalties from the books he writes and no remuneration from Desiring God. These funds are all reinvested into our gospel-spreading efforts. DG also has a whatever-you-can-afford policy for the materials we sell, designed for individuals with limited discretionary funds. If you'd like more information about this policy, please contact us at the address or phone number below.

We exist to help you treasure Jesus Christ above all things because he is most glorified in you when you are most satisfied in him. Let us know how we can serve you!

---

**Desiring God**
2601 East Franklin Avenue
Minneapolis, MN 55406-1103

888.346.4700 (phone)
612.338.4372 (fax)
Email: mail@desiringGod.org
Web: www.desiringGod.org